ONE HOLY
HUNGER

Discovering the God
You've Never Known

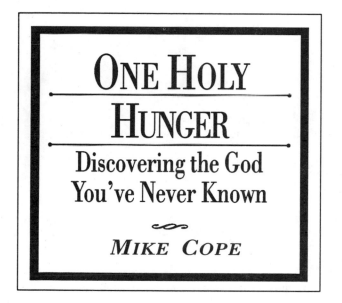

ONE HOLY
HUNGER
Discovering the God
You've Never Known

MIKE COPE

— *A* —
FAITH*FOCUS*
Book

Sweet Publishing
Fort Worth, Texas

One Holy Hunger
Discovering the God You've Never Known

Cover: Terry Dugan Design

Library of Congress Catalog Number 93-85142

ISBN: 0-8344-0231-9

Printed in the U. S. A.
10 9 8 7 6 5 4 3 2

To Matthew
Megan
and
Christopher

Special gifts from God—
a God who longs for your
three precious hearts!

Contents

WE HUNGER FOR GOD AND DON'T EVEN KNOW IT

1. *One Holy Hunger...*   1
   Expecting More Than People Can Give

2. *One Holy Hunger...*   17
   Searching for Self-Esteem and
   Significance

3. *One Holy Hunger...*   33
   Yearning for Love and Compassion

4. *One Holy Hunger...*   47
   Longing for More in My Marriage

5. *One Holy Hunger...*   59
   Seeking Security and Safety

WE'RE STARVING TO DEATH FROM FALSE IDEAS ABOUT GOD

6. *False Idea...*   71
   God Wants Me to Be Afraid of Him

7. *False Idea...*   83
   God Is Going to Zap Me

8. *False Idea . . .*   93
    God Never Comes Through

9. *False Idea . . .*   105
    God Loves Me Only When I'm Good

10. *False Idea . . .*   119
    Even God Can't Fix My Mess

DARE TO DISCOVER THE LIVING GOD

11. *Discover. . .*   135
    The Approachable King

12. *Discover. . .*   151
    The God Who Changes the
    Unchangeable

13. *Discover. . .*   163
    The Perfect Imprint of God

PART 1:

WE HUNGER FOR GOD AND DON'T EVEN KNOW IT

*Blessed are those who hunger and thirst
for righteousness,
for they will be filled.*

*Blessed are the pure in heart,
for they will see God.*

Matthew 5:6, 8

Chapter 1

One Holy Hunger:

Expecting More

Than People

Can Give

$\mathbf{A}$s I write, my ears give life an A+ but my calf muscles are offering nothing higher than a D–. That's because earlier today I went down (and up!) the Bright Angel Trail into the Grand Canyon.

> **Discovery:**
>
> *Only God can satisfy my hunger for perfect relationships.*

My ears think life is great, because they are listening to Susan Ashton's sweet voice singing her hit song "Grand Canyon." Every time I hear the song, I identify with the lyrics. I've experienced these moments when God has calmed "the waters raging in the river of my mind." I remember well hours of ecstasy when I've felt as close to God as a shadow. And, on the other hand, I've been through times when I've felt distant from my Creator—like I'm "looking up at [him] from the bottom of the Grand Canyon."

My calves, however, are ready to give up on life because they are aching from hours of hiking. Even though my legs are complaining, the song means more than ever. As I hear Ashton sing "there's a Grand Canyon between you and me," I'm aware tonight just how enormous that distance can be.

That gap between us and God leaves us spiritually dehydrated—feeling on the inside like some of the weary hikers looked on the outside as they neared the rim of God's Big Hole. And, just as many of them rushed to the water fountain that awaited them like a gold ribbon on the top, so we develop a spiritual thirst for pure, clear, eternal water.

It's a thirst you might find in a crowded office on the sixteenth floor of a downtown office building. Or in a lonely kitchen that is full of utensils, but empty of joy. Or on a back row at a church assembly. Or even . . . in a bar.

Eleven years of situation comedy in a Boston bar came to an end in 1993 when the "Cheers" gang circled up for a discussion of what life is all about. Sam "May-Day" Malone moaned that one by one he seemed to be losing his thrills and tingles: "I keep asking myself, what is the point of life?"

Cliff, the dedicated mail carrier and master of trivia, suggested that the key to real life is comfortable shoes. He offered as historical support Aristotle (sandals), Confucius (thongs), and Einstein (loose loafers).

Carla, the barracuda barmaid, then gave her opinion: the greatest goal of life is having children. But in her brief reflections on child-rearing difficulties, she talked herself out of the suggestion.

Finally, Norm, the unemployed, almost permanent fixture there, felt that the key to life is love—

especially his love for his barstool.
"What is the point of life?" Sam wanted to know.
It's a question many don't even bother to ask.

Doing Time

Most people rarely even consider their purpose.
Some of us tend to think that if we stay very busy, if
our Daytimer calendars are full, we must be purposeful. What *is* life all about? It's a hard question. It is
much easier to ignore it than to answer it.

One reason people don't spend much time thinking about their lives is because it doesn't seem to
matter. Like the commercial, "Why ask why?" Life is
fine. Too many of us live from weekend to weekend,
worshiping the American god TGIF. We have children, go to the mall, take vacations every third year,
and stash away a few bucks for retirement. Everything seems pretty good. But this is moving through
life at warp speed without a rearview mirror to
reflect on the past or a front windshield to make sure
we're going the right way. In other words, we're just
doing time. We don't have any idea where we are
going, but we want to get there fast. It's a pointless
way to live.

Another factor that sometimes holds us back from
considering our life is fear. Most of us are a little
afraid to meditate on our lives, fearful of what we
will conclude. We hunger for something we don't
want to acknowledge.

That's why, like the characters on "Cheers,"
people don't actually ask this question until they are
facing the end. This can be the end of an era, like
when we graduate from college or retire, or experience extreme adversity such as illness or death.
Unfortunately, even when we allow ourselves to

consider life, we often come up feeling empty. This is because the world does not have an answer to the question. The wisdom of the world tells each of us we must search and find our own purpose. This leads people on an endless, futile search for meaning.

How have people fared from following the wisdom of the world? Check it out: broken relationships, scarred lives, domestic violence, emptiness and loneliness, shattered dreams, substance abuse, and abandoned children. Christians are facing these pressing problems like everyone else.

Yet in a deeper sense, these aren't so much the problems as they are some symptoms of a larger problem!

But God still loves us and longs to be in relationship with us.

The larger problem is that we ignore the fact that we were made to live in relationship with God. When we ignore or minimize that need for a relationship we become like fish trying to live on land or humans trying to live on a planet that has no oxygen.

If Jesus were given a chance at Cheers to offer his purpose of life, I think he'd have two messages. First, he would say that God loves us deeply, just as we are. Our bodies may not be proportioned right, our marriages may be in shambles, we may be guilty of shameful sins. But God still loves us and longs to be in relationship with us.

Secondly, Jesus would tell those drifting characters that life does have a purpose. Their hunger can be satisfied—not by people, possessions, or money— but only by being filled with God's presence and having a relationship with him.

Understanding Our Hunger

One reason we may not recognize our hunger for God is because we Americans don't know what hunger really is. During the famine in Somalia, thousands of starving families left their homes and once-productive farms to seek shelter and food at distant refugee centers. Foreign nations and humanitarian agencies sent and distributed food to these starving people. Many received help in time to save their lives. Some, however, waited too long before seeking help. They were so malnourished that when they tried to eat, their bodies rejected food. Their digestive systems had shut down and would no longer process the very thing their bodies needed. Many died because their bodies no longer recognized or accepted life-sustaining nourishment. Their bodies didn't recognize what they were hungering for.

The psalmist had a deep hunger, but unlike most folks, he understood the source of his hunger and expressed it clearly:

> As a deer longs for flowing streams,
>   so my soul longs for you, O God.
> My soul thirsts for God,
>   for the living God.
>   Psalm 42:1, 2a (NRSV)

You can hear the grumbling caused by hunger pains all around from bars to Bible classes. Unfortunately, people—both those outside the church and many inside—have failed to recognize in those hunger pains a deep longing for God.

Many people identify their hunger as the need for a relationship, which it is. But they look for the perfect relationship with another person. They try to fill their void with a parent, spouse, or child. They endlessly look for that someone who can make them happy and complete. Each time they are disappointed because there are no perfect human relationships. There is no person that can make you or me feel satisfied.

Only God can bring fulfillment to our lives—because he made us to live in harmony with him. Scripture never tells us to love another person with all our heart, soul, mind, and strength. That is investing way too much in any human being. The place to invest our heart, soul, mind, and strength is with God, and God alone.

There is no person that can make
you or me feel satisfied.

Notice these testimonies from people who invested in God and hungered for him:

You have made us for yourself, and our souls are restless until they rest in you.
                                        Augustine

Your name and renown
    are the desire of our hearts.
My soul yearns for you in the night;
    in the morning my spirit longs for you.
                              Isaiah 26:8b, 9

Made as we were in the image of God, we scarcely find it strange to take again our God as

our all. God was our original habitat and our
hearts cannot but feel at home when they enter
again that ancient and beautiful abode.[1]

O God, you are my God,
earnestly I seek you;
my soul thirsts for you,
my body longs for you,
in a dry and weary land
where there is no water.
Psalm 63:1

Each of these testimonies cuts through the noise
of culture to hear the one clear voice of God—a God
who created us, sent his Son for us, and longs for us
intensely. And, he carefully made each of us with an
inner desire—a hunger—to know him. His heart
rejoices when we accept and draw near to him. He
delights when we accept his eager desire for a relationship with us.

Yet the LORD longs to be gracious to you;
he rises to show you compassion.
For the LORD is a God of justice.
Blessed are all who wait for him!
Isaiah 30:18

God is a self-sufficient God and needs nothing,
including us, to be complete. Yet, he loves us so
much, so overwhelmingly, and he wants us to benefit
from his abundant blessings. So he relentlessly
pursues us as a shepherd for his sheep, as a father
for his child, as a mother for her baby, as a groom for
his bride.

Until we understand that and respond to his love,
we are like the prodigal son, searching again for the
security of our home. And our search will end in

disappointment until we search for God. No human relationship, no job, no possession, and no amount of money or success can ultimately satisfy us.

God Hunger

Our hunger is for God. Not God as a doctrine . . . or as an idea . . . or as the necessary conclusion of our "proofs." But God as a living Being. As a Someone who pursues a relationship—with us!

> *We easily fall into the trap of*
> *believing that information is the key*
> *to eternal life.*

For those of us with a Christian heritage this seems so obvious. But there are a couple of problems we as Christians face—barriers that can easily sidetrack us in our response to God, barriers that keep us from realizing we are *all* God-hungry and that only he can fill us.

Barrier One: Our Confusion

One problem is our tendency to confuse **knowledge about God** with **knowing God**. We easily fall into the trap of believing that information is the key to eternal life. So we turn to "data-based Christianity" to fill us with knowledge about God. We then open the pages of Scripture to memorize events that can later be regurgitated as if Christian living were similar to a sophomore history class. What happened on the fifth day of Creation? Who were Moses' parents? Who was the second judge? What objects were in the ark of the covenant? How many chapters are in the Book of Psalms?

We can buzz through the Old Testament without ever pausing to ask, "What is the message of Scripture? What is its central point? What is it trying to accomplish?" As a result, we can become proficient in biblical information without becoming closer to God and more sensitive to the people he has created.

Don't misunderstand me: I'm all in favor of learning the information of Scripture. Biblical illiteracy isn't a virtue! But biblical knowledge shouldn't be the goal of our reading. Scripture was written to reveal to us a God who longs for relationships. It pleads with us to long for him as well. The goal of Scripture isn't minds filled with facts about God but hearts that are using those facts to be full of his presence.

Their hunger is not a mere physical or emotional hunger. It is a holy hunger—a hunger from God for God.

I remember reading about Dennis Wise, a young man who spent all his time collecting Elvis memorabilia: clothes, records, photographs, programs. He even underwent plastic surgery to try to look more like his hero. But his great regret was that he never got to meet the man he adored.

A similar but much greater tragedy with many Christians is that they spend years listening to sermons, reading Scripture, and teaching Sunday school classes but fail to enjoy an intimate relationship with God. They could pass any theological exam or answer any Bible trivia question. But they don't hunger and thirst to know God personally, to be filled with his presence, to be changed into his likeness. No wonder religion often becomes empty!

Barrier Two: Our Satisfaction

A second problem we face is that we're too easily satisfied. We're like the toddler who could wait and have a wonderful meal at 6:00 but who finds an old hot dog from lunch on the floor at 5:40 and gobbles it down. We are offered a fabulous vacation by the ocean and settle instead for wading in a ditch.

Instead of craving a vibrant relationship with the God who made us, we settle for a house, a family, a few friends, a job, a TV and VCR, and a yearly vacation. We think we can survive with this and just a bit of religion. Yet our souls starve!

Frederick Buechner, author and theologian, tells of a twelve year old who, in a fit of rage, killed his father. Later a guard was walking down the hall where the boy was being held and heard him whimpering. When he neared the door to the youngster's room, he heard him crying, "I want my father. I want my father."

That is the sobbing that can be heard all around us—even though people may not know what or whom they are crying for. But the things we accumulate in life can't satisfy us and can't give us purpose.

Longing for God

People who are trying to fill their hunger for love, acceptance, and security in relationships, material possessions, or even success will never find real or lasting satisfaction.

Their hunger is not a mere physical or emotional

hunger. It is a holy hunger—a hunger from God for God. Some may not know they long for him because they don't know him. Some don't seek him because they don't know where or how to look. Others are looking for God, but they aren't sure what he "looks like."

For a couple of years in the early 1990s, the _New York Times_ Bestseller List included picture books starring a funny little man named Waldo. In _Where's Waldo?_ and its sequels the object is to find the little guy amidst all the other people and objects. Sometimes he blends into the background, while at other times he "hides" in the foreground. Waldo is easily recognizable because he has specific physical characteristics that never change. However, clutter and things around him often obscure and confuse the reader's vision. Though a reader may sometimes give up, assuming there was a trick page that omits Waldo just to drive you crazy, he's there every time.

Even when he's silent, however,
he is not absent.

That's Scripture's testimony about God—he is there every time. Sometimes God is so present you can't miss him—like when he brought fire down on the altar at Mount Carmel in 1 Kings 18. But at other times he seems hidden—as when he was present in the whisper in 1 Kings 19. Even when he's silent, however, he is not absent.

Let's return to Scripture and hear God's testimony about himself. The Bible is a thrilling story of a God who cannot possibly be fully understood but who nevertheless invites us to share his life. Since our

minds are so limited in understanding this Eternal
One, this God has offered metaphors and descriptions that permit us to catch a glimpse of his Being.

Taste God's Goodness

The goal, of course, isn't for us to read this and
then be able to list the qualities of God or the biblical
metaphors that refer to God. Rather, the goal is to
know God better. This is a plea for us to "taste and
see that the LORD is good," as Psalm 34:8 invites us.
Rather than reading a list of ingredients in home-
made chocolate ice cream, isn't it better just to eat a
bowl . . . or two? So, rather than just filling our
minds with facts about God, we're invited to fill our
hearts with *him*.

*Rather than just filling our minds
with facts about God, we're invited to
fill our hearts with* him.

A couple of decades ago, J. I. Packer wrote in his
classic book, *Knowing God*, that "we must seek, in
studying God, to be led to God." We seek to know
him by praying, by crying out, by meditating, by
trusting when we've been afraid to trust, by submit-
ting, by obeying.

A doorman at a Broadway theater was asked if
during his nineteen years there he enjoyed the
shows that had come through. His answer was
startling: he hadn't been interested, so he'd never
gone in where the performance was.

How long have you been just outside the door
which God has opened for you? How long have you

tried to quench your thirst with brackish water or
satisfy your hunger with worthless junk food? As the
following writers tell us, all we have to do is open
the door and let God strengthen us:

> Whom have I in heaven but you?
>   And earth has nothing I desire
>   besides you.
> My flesh and my heart may fail,
>   but God is the strength of my heart
>   and my portion forever.
> Psalm 73:25, 26

O God, I have tasted thy goodness, and it has
both satisfied me and made me thirsty for more.
I am painfully conscious of my need of further
grace. I am ashamed of my lack of desire. O God,
the Triune God, I want to want Thee; I long to be
filled with longing; I thirst to be made more
thirsty still.[2]

_____

Notes

1. A. W. Tozer, *The Pursuit of God* (Camp Hill, Pennsylvania:
Christian Publications, Inc., 1982).

2. Ibid.

Focusing Your Faith

1. What is the one hunger which causes you the greatest pain in your daily living—a relationship, security, success, possessions?

2. How does it make you feel to hear that God created that hunger in you for your benefit?

3. When was the last time you thought about life and its purpose?

4. If you and your friends sat down to discuss life, what would your conclusions be?

5. What "junk food" solutions have you been using to try to ease your hunger for God?

6. Like in *The Great Waldo Search*, what has been cluttering your clear view of God? Where have you been looking for him?

7. How do you visualize God from all that you've learned about him? Is your picture of him smiling or frowning?

Chapter 2

One Holy Hunger:

Searching for
Self-Esteem and
Significance

As we arrived at
our son's second grade
classroom for open
house my wife Diane
and I were greeted by
his teacher, who urged
us to read the poster
prepared by our child
and displayed just
outside the door. She
had asked each of the
children to write three sentences that described who
they were and what they liked. That'll be interesting, we thought. We searched for the familiar script
that said MATT. His lines read:

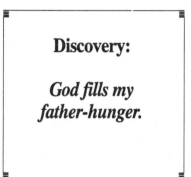

Discovery:

*God fills my
father-hunger.*

> I am in second grade.
> I like to play baseball.
> I am a cool dude.

What would possess a kid to write that he was a

cool dude? we laughed. That's when we noticed that this was the last sentence on every boy's poster—obviously a case of a good idea out of control. The only difference was that some had made a spelling error and had written "I am a cool dud"—an interesting contradiction in terms!

***Like it or not, each person bears the
indelible stamp of a father.***

The teacher also urged us to read the sentences on the children's desks. She had begun three sentences and had asked them to complete them—again, so that we could gain understanding about our kids. She had written, "When I'm by myself I like to . . ." Matt wrote, ". . . look at my baseball cards." Then she had, "When I'm with my friends I like to . . ." My son said, ". . . trade baseball cards." Finally, she had put, "When I'm with my dad I like to . . ." Matt wrote, ". . . buy baseball cards."

I'm glad he finds Dad good for something—if for nothing more than the one who'll spring for a pack of Topps.

Like it or not, each person bears the indelible stamp of a father, a person whose impact we rarely escape. The popular 1991 film *City Slickers* portrays this inescapable impact. In the movie, three urban men are trying to deal with midlife crisis by participating in a cattle drive. In one important scene the three are quizzing each other about the best and worst days of their lives. For each of them, a father was at the center. For one, the best day was when he was seven and his dad took him to Yankee stadium. For another, the best day was when he married. He

told how his dad winked at him during the ceremony, as if to say, "You're a man now." And for the
third, the best—and worst—day was when he told
his father to get out of the house because he was
hurting the family through his infidelity.

Father Hunger

Ken Druck and James Simmons in _The Secrets
Men Keep_ discuss six major secrets men have. At the
top of the list is that "men secretly yearn for their
father's love and approval." This is (often without
their conscious knowledge) behind the drive many
males have to prove themselves. In it they say:

It may surprise us to know that the most powerful
common denominator influencing men's lives today
is the relationship we had with our fathers. . . . Of
the hundreds of men I have surveyed over the
years, perhaps 90 percent admitted they still had
strings leading back to their fathers. In other
words, they are still looking to their fathers, even
though their fathers may have been dead for years,
for approval, acceptance, affection, and understanding.[1]

But men aren't the only ones with a yearning for
their fathers. In her book _Like Father, Like Daughter: How Father Shapes the Woman His Daughter
Becomes_, Suzanne Fields presents the results of her
interviews with hundreds of women. The central
thesis of her research was "Daddy hides, and we
forever seek him, only occasionally flushing him out
of his hiding places."

This "father hunger" doesn't end with a desire for
the man who was the biological parent. It is a craving

for the affirmation, affection, discipline, protection, leadership, and unconditional acceptance that should come from a dad.

When Scripture says that God is like a father and that he is, in fact, our Father, it is telling us that these needs can be met. But not by a flesh-and-blood being, because no matter how wonderful a human model is, he falls short. There are no perfect earthly dads.

Starving for Affection

Some may find it hard to get excited about the scriptural descriptions of God as a father because of the imperfect models of fatherhood they have experienced here on earth.

Some remember a father who was too wrapped up in his job, his buddies, and his hobbies to provide much support or affirmation. He might have been one of those deluded men who believed that their only job was to "provide" (to bring home a paycheck), while Mom was responsible for everything else. I remember a college student telling me that he would gladly have settled for fewer material possessions if his dad would have just come to his ball games or watched a movie with him once in a while.

Others recall a father who abandoned them. A good friend of mine, an elementary school principal, was asked to speak with a third grader who, though a good student, was performing poorly and was whimpering all day. When he asked the eight year old why he couldn't concentrate on his lessons, the boy said, "I'm afraid that when school's over, my mom won't pick me up because she'll have left me." Michael replied, "Your mama wouldn't do that." The boy's head lowered as he muttered, "My dad did."

After my friend promised that the boy could go home with him if his mother didn't show up, the youngster was fine. His immediate fears of being left alone were alleviated. But how many other children have to spend years thinking about a dad who walked out? And you say God is a father?

Our search for a father will
never end until we see God as our
only perfect father.

Others choke back the memories of a father who was harsh—maybe even verbally or physically abusive. The tragedy of child abuse is common beyond belief—even in homes which claim to be Christian! Dozens of times I've talked with students who wince at the thought that God is like a father, because they were abused—often sexually—in their "Christian" homes.

Where can people turn for the affirmation, guidance, security, and acceptance that a father should provide? Where can we look for someone who can help us build our self-esteem? In the eighth century B.C., Hosea spoke to God a message that resonates today: "In you the fatherless find compassion" (14:3). Our search for a father will never end until we see God as our only perfect father.

The Biblical Portrait

Even though we think of the fatherhood of God as a New Testament teaching, there are several occurrences of this theme in the Old Testament. For example:

Out of Egypt I called my son (Hosea 11:1).

O Lord, you are our Father (Isaiah 64:8).

I am Israel's father, and Ephraim is my firstborn son (Jeremiah 31:9).

It is in the New Testament where the imagery blossoms, however. While Jews in the synagogue might pray "Our Father, our King," there are no instances found in first century Palestine of a Jew saying just "our Father." This revolutionary picture came from Jesus. In John alone, he refers over 100 times to God as Father. He taught us to pray, "Our Father in heaven" (Matthew 6:9).

Paul developed the beautiful picture by describing our adoption by God the Father:

> For you did not receive a spirit that makes you a slave again to fear, but you received the Spirit of sonship. And by him we cry, "*Abba*, Father." The Spirit himself testifies with our spirit that we are God's children. Now if we are children, then we are heirs—heirs of God and co-heirs with Christ, if indeed we share in his sufferings in order that we may also share in his glory (Romans 8:15-17).

> Because you are sons, God sent the Spirit of his Son into our hearts, the Spirit who calls out, "*Abba*, Father." So you are no longer a slave, but a son; and since you are a son, God has made you also an heir (Galatians 4:6, 7).

God has chosen us, adopted us, despite all our failures. Adoption agencies tell us it is much easier for them to find a home for a healthy baby than one with physical handicaps. But thankfully God didn't adopt us because we were healthy. He chose us

because of his unconditional love. Through Jesus
Christ we became his sons and daughters.

---

*God has chosen us, adopted us,
despite all our failures.*

How does this description of God as a father help
us understand him? What does it communicate
about how he relates to us?

A Loving Relationship

First, the description of God as a father communi-
cates a loving, accepting relationship. In Hosea 11,
God explains to his wayward child, "When Israel
was a child, I loved him" (v. 1). He continues with
the sentimental language of parenting: "It was I who
taught Ephraim to walk, taking them by the arms"
(v. 3). God is like the thirty year old coaxing his
toddler along while he tries to steady the video
camera, catching those first smiles, first steps, and
first words. But the relationship between God and
Israel was built solely upon God's love, not on the
wonder or majesty of Israel.

Christian author Philip Yancey has written about
a time on a holiday visit with his mother when he
pulled down a large box of old photos from the closet.
It contained shots of him in cowboy and Indian
costumes, in a Peter Cottontail suit for a first-grade
play, and in cap and gown for graduation.

What captured his attention that day, however,
was a typical "infant shot": a fat cheeked, half-bald
baby, with an unfocused look to the eyes. But the
picture was crumpled and mangled. Why, he asked
his mother, would she hold on to this old photo when
there were so many others in much better condition?

She explained that when he was ten months old, his father contracted spinal lumbar polio, totally paralyzing him and forcing him, at the age of twenty-four, to live inside an iron lung. All he asked for was a picture of his wife and two sons. She had managed to cram that old photo between the metal knobs on the large steel cylinder that did his breathing for him. Philip's father spent three months there until he died, staring at the son whom he hardly knew but deeply loved. Yancey writes:

> I have often thought of that crumpled photo, for it is one of the few links connecting me to the stranger who was my father. Someone I have no memory of, no sensory knowledge of, spent all day every day thinking of me, devoting himself to me, loving me as well as he could.
>
> I mention this story because the emotions I felt when my mother showed me the crumpled photo were the very same emotions I felt that February night in a college dorm room when I first believed in a God of love. Someone is there, I realized. Someone is watching life as it unfolds on this planet. More, Someone is there who loves me. It was a startling feeling of wild hope, a feeling so new and overwhelming that it seemed fully worth risking my life on.[2]

The powerful language of love created by this paternal portrait of God is a language I, too, am fortunate to understand. When my family made a trip to Austin, Texas, during my teenage years, my mom showed me the second-story apartment where we lived while she and my dad were attending the University of Texas. She told me about the day I slipped out the door, squeezed through the guardrail, and fell. When my dad found me screaming on the pavement below with blood streaming from my head, he flew down the stairs to get me. Not knowing how seriously I might be hurt, he decided I must get to a hospital fast. He could call a taxi or an ambulance, but who knows how long they might take to arrive? So my father scooped me up in his arms and ran with me to the hospital. (I'm lucky, I guess, that he's always been a great runner!)

Now that I'm a father, I can begin to comprehend even better the portrait of wild love painted by this fatherly picture. What else but limitless love would make me want to cross the country through the night on a "red-eye special" just to sit in the stands on a Saturday morning to watch a seven year old kick a soccer ball? Why else would I look into a classroom of children who are mentally handicapped and spot only one precious girl? This isn't a love my kids have earned; I loved them from the moment I knew they were conceived!

What a staggering thought! You are of such great concern to the God of the universe! Even though he watches over billions of people, he is able to spot you in a crowd—because you're his child, and he loves you.

A Demanding Relationship

The comfort that stems from the love God brings to this relationship is quickly matched by the challenge before us—to respond, as every child should, with trust and obedience.

As parents we hope that our children will trust us. You can imagine the small girl as she inches toward the swimming pool where her father awaits with outstretched arms. He urges her to leap in. "I know it's over your head, but I'll catch you." She surveys the depths once more, closes her eyes, and springs toward this man to whom she has just entrusted her life.

As parents we also insist that our children obey us. We set limits because we love them, and we don't want to see them get hurt. "I know the street is a great place to play ball. I understand that it's nice and wide and that the ball bounces better on it. But you could be hurt badly by a car."

Because of his great love for us, God has insisted that we allow him to guide us.

We don't want to see them in pain—partly because we always feel their pain so deeply. When Matt was still a little guy of about five years old, he had the third surgery to put tubes in his ears. The man who takes blood (whom we affectionately called "the bloodsucker") entered our room. As he stuck the needle in my son and began to draw out the blood, he warned me that after he left I'd need to make sure Matt sat down because he might faint if he didn't. I kept staring at that long needle and the blood flowing out of my son's arm as he told me again to be sure he didn't pass out. Then he yanked the needle out, slowly wiped off the tip, and walked out. As he left, he turned and said, "Don't forget. Someone could faint." Just after he shut the door his prophecy came true: someone did faint. But it wasn't Matt. He was fine. I, however, was out. I'd have been fine if the blood had come out of my own arm, but I couldn't endure the pain I thought my child must be enduring.

Because of his great love for us, God has insisted

that we allow him to guide us. He has graciously offered us instruction on how to live. While his guidelines may at times seem like oppressive restrictions, they are intended to protect us from pain.

Imagine God's deep hurt, then, when he cries out that his child Israel refused to trust or obey him:

> But the more I called Israel,
>   the further they went from me.
> They sacrificed to the Baals
>   and they burned incense to images.
> It was I who taught Ephraim to walk,
>   taking them by the arms;
> but they did not realize
>   it was I who healed them.
> I led them with cords of human kindness,
>   with ties of love;
> I lifted the yoke from their neck
>   and bent down to feed them.
> Will they not return to Egypt
>   and will not Assyria rule over them
>   because they refuse to repent?
> Swords will flash in their cities,
>   will destroy the bars of their gates
>   and put an end to their plans.
> My people are determined to turn from me.
>   Hosea 11:2-7a

This is the same agony God expresses in Jeremiah when he mourns, "I thought you would call me 'Father' and not turn away from following me" (3:19) and in Malachi when he asks, "If I am a father, where is the honor due me?" (1:6).

A Relentless Relationship

If we fail in our obedient trust, is all hope

destroyed? It certainly sounds like it. By all expectations God should be sick of Israel (and with us)
because of persistent failures to follow him. But
parents don't give up very easily!

A few times, I've had the task of counseling
parents whose children completely rebelled, even to
the point of winding up in prison. No matter how
much I might insist that they need to practice "tough
love" by letting their children reap what they've
sown, most parents cannot turn loose. It's easier to
make pronouncements about what should be done
when it's not your son or daughter, they have told
me. And I am beginning to see how that must be
true. A parent's love is relentless. No matter what
my children might do, I would always want them
back.

Right after saying that Israel had gone too far
and was going to face destruction, the fatherliness of
God breaks out:

> How can I give you up, Ephraim?
>   How can I hand you over, Israel?
> How can I treat you like Admah?
>   How can I make you like Zeboiim?
> My heart is changed within me;
>   all my compassion is aroused.
> I will not carry out my fierce anger,
>   nor will I turn and devastate Ephraim.
> For I am God, and not man—
>   the Holy One among you.
>   Hosea 11:8, 9

According to Hosea, this relationship, this covenant, is rooted in the steadfast love of God. He is a
father who anxiously awaits the return of any prodigal son or daughter, no matter how far from home

they may have wandered (Luke 15).

Filling the Father Hunger

We are living in a time when "father hunger" seems like a national epidemic. No human father can ever provide us with all we need. Even the best can't give us the leadership, affection, protection, and unconditional acceptance we crave.

This God-given hunger will continue until we realize that God is the ultimate good Father for whom we desperately search. It is only in him that we can find our self-esteem and significance. We will be forever searching, forever restless until we rest in him!

Notes:

1. Ken Druck and James Simmons, _The Secrets Men Keep_ (New York: Ballantine, a division of Random House, 1985).
2. Philip Yancey, _Campus Life_ (January 1989): 50. Used by permission.

Focusing Your Faith

1. Write three short statements that describe who you are and what you like.

2. What is/was your relationship with your father like? Have you received all the love and affirmation that should come from a dad?

3. How do you think your image of God has been influenced by your father?

4. If God is the perfect Father, why did he turn away from Jesus on the cross? How does that make you feel about yourself?

5. Is it difficult for you to feel special and loved by God? Why or why not?

6. As you make difficult decisions from day to day, what advice do you "hear" your father give you most often? What would your heavenly Father say about that advice?

7. Write a prayer to reaffirm your security and self-esteem in your Father.

Chapter 3

One Holy Hunger:

Yearning for
Love and
Compassion

Thinking of God as a father is not a new concept. We have heard it, read it, and even sung it. While we are comfortable with talking about God as a father, many of us may break out in a sweat at the suggestion that he is also like a mother.

Discovery:

God provides the perfect mother-love.

But I assure you this chapter isn't an attempt to be politically correct; rather, it is an attempt to be biblically precise. As Oswald Chambers has written, "The mothering affection of God is revealed all through the Old Testament." Besides saying that God is like a mother, Scripture compares him to a mother eagle, a lioness, a womb that gives birth, and a mother hen watching over her chicks.

Keep in mind that we're working with metaphors:

God is a father, a mother, a shepherd, a king, a fire, a shield, a rock. These words provide comparisons for us to help us understand who this Almighty One is and what he's like. Each image has its limitations, of course. For example, there are ways in which God is like a father and other ways in which he's not. Our task is to discover what range of associations, out of the many possibilities, is intended to tell us about God.

God clearly is neither male nor female.

Much of our discomfort in comparing God to a mother is that we have tended to conceive of God as a male—even though God clearly is neither male nor female. Scripture helps us understand God by using both masculine and feminine language. Even when he's called a father, we're dealing with a metaphor. God is not a flesh-and-blood male! But the language of fatherhood evokes many truths that are appropriate to who God is and to the nature of our relationship with him.

It is important not to ignore or "explain away" the feminine metaphors. An English professor I know who is an avid student of medieval literature believes that the worship of Mary in the Catholic church stems largely from centuries of failure to study and appreciate these feminine metaphors. The church has been left with a lopsided, masculine picture of God—a picture that tended to be too strict for anyone to endure. They needed Mary as an avenue to express the godly traits of compassion, acceptance, and nurturing.

Lovingly Intimate

When we study the mothering side of God, we discover a God who yearns for intimacy with us. This Holy One longs to be close to his people as a mother longs to be with her child.

Here is an area where Mom has a distinct advantage over Dad. For nine months a child is sheltered in a warm, safe, cozy place. It's the most secure life ever gets!

The day the child meets Dad is the worst day of his life! He has to squeeze through the birth canal until he looks like a conehead. Then someone spanks him to make him cry. Talk about a rotten day! But then the child decides he may survive when someone hands him back to Mom and he is able to nurse. Again, he is close and secure.

This picture of comfort and intimacy is painted in the last chapter of Isaiah when God speaks of his people returning from exile. It is a beautiful portrait of Mother Zion receiving her children:

> Before she goes into labor,
>   she gives birth;
> before the pains come upon her,
>   she delivers a son.
> Who has ever heard of such a thing?
>   Who has ever seen such things?
> Can a country be born in a day
>   or a nation be brought forth in a
>   moment?
> Yet no sooner is Zion in labor
>   than she gives birth to her children.
>   Isaiah 66:7, 8

Then the comparison changes, however, and God becomes the mother comforting her children:

> As a mother comforts her child,
>   so will I comfort you;
>   and you will be comforted over
>   Jerusalem.
>   Isaiah 66:13

Aching to Be Near

In Psalm 131, the psalmist compares our relationship to God to that of a weaned child with its mother:

> My heart is not proud, O LORD,
>   my eyes are not haughty;
> I do not concern myself with great matters
>   or things too wonderful for me.
> But I have stilled and quieted my soul;
>   like a weaned child with its mother,
>   like a weaned child is my soul within me.
> O Israel, put your hope in the LORD
>   both now and forevermore (vv. 1-3).

Prior to weaning, there are many reasons a child might want to be with Mom, but most of them have to do with what she can provide. She is the great Supplier of Needs. Sometimes Mom is, in a word, LUNCH.

A weaned child, however, learns to be satisfied in merely being with her mother. It's often very different with Dad. When I come home, it's time to wrestle, throw a ball, or play games. But often I see our children plop down on the couch just to be near their mother.

Just as a child learns to enjoy Mom's presence without hoping to get something from her, so also a child of God aches for God's presence. We long for moments to be with him, to sense his nearness—not

because of what he can give us but because of who
he is.

*We long for moments to be with him,
to sense his nearness.*

The weaned relationship is a restful one. As
contemporary Christian author Eugene Peterson has
put it, "Christian faith is not neurotic dependence
but childlike trust. We do not have a God who forever indulges our whims but a God whom we trust
with our destinies."

Fiercely Protective

The language of motherhood evokes not only the
thought of intimacy but also the idea of protection.
God is a fierce protector of his children: God is a bear
whose cubs have been taken away (Hosea 13:8), an
eagle guarding her nest (Deuteronomy 32:11), and a
hen brooding over her chicks (Matthew 23:37).

I still have the "mothering" instructions left by
my wife as she was preparing to go out of town. This
flurry of instructions was to make sure our three-
year-old son and our infant daughter were properly
cared for while she was gone:

Ask what kind of sandwich he wants. He'll say
"ham and cheese." Give him bologna and cheese.
He doesn't know the difference. Make him half a
sandwich. He'll say he wants two. So cut it in
half. He won't know the difference. Ask what he
wants on it. He'll say "mustard and mayonnaise."
Be sure not to put them on the same piece of
bread or he won't eat it. Feed Megan her cereal.

She's hungry. Just because she isn't crying yet doesn't mean she isn't hungry. Be patient with her. Just because she's slow doesn't mean she's full. Just use your own judgment.

Whew! My head was spinning. The best line, of course was the last: "Just use your own judgment." My own judgment was the very thing she was trying to avoid! She wanted me to use her judgment, because Mom knows how to care, protect, and guard.

A powerful example of a mother's protective instincts came recently to public prominence. Dr. Elizabeth Morgan, a renowned surgeon, author, and graduate of Harvard and Yale, spent a couple of years in prison in Washington, D.C., to protect her six-year-old daughter from rape.

Into whose hands do we commit our spirits?

When her daughter, Hilary, was still a toddler, she began to exhibit signs of sexual abuse by her father, Dr. Morgan's ex-husband. Thirteen doctors and psychiatrists examined the girl, and eleven concluded that she had indeed been abused. But when the judge studied the evidence, his opinion was that it was inconclusive. He ordered that she spend a two-week visit with her father—an unsupervised visit!

Convinced that this was court-sanctioned abuse, Dr. Morgan sent her daughter into hiding. For about two years she shared a 6' x 11' cell with criminals because of her "contempt of court." She sacrificed her medical practice, her savings, and her liberty to protect her child.

This same protective nature of God is highlighted when Scripture calls him our rock, our shield, our fortress, our hiding place, and our shelter. God is the one who never abandons us in times of danger. He protects us in our sufferings.

Everyone has moments growing up when they want to curl up in a fetal position and call out, "I want my mommy!" Scripture is telling us there is One like a mother whom we can come to, One who will surround us with loving protection.

When Jesus hung on the cross, he cried, "Into your hands I commit my spirit" (Luke 23:46). A challenging question for us is: Into whose hands do we commit _our_ spirits? When we face aging parents, endangered marriages, rebellious children, financial problems, frightening symptoms, unexpected diagnoses, embarrassing pasts, or unsure futures, into whose hands will we commit our lives?

Endlessly Devoted

A third idea suggested by the language of motherhood is that of endless devotion. Last spring my daughter had a case of chicken pox that could be listed in the _Guinness Book of World Records_. Every square inch of her body (eyes included!) was covered. After a couple of days she was a pathetic looking little girl: her hair was matted, her face had gunk all over it, and her eyes were swollen shut. She walked around the house with her arms outstretched, seeking someone to hold her. My son Matt and I learned that if we'd freeze she couldn't find us! But my wife Diane was always willing to hold her. I will never forget the picture of mother holding daughter, rocking for endless hours.

When no one else will receive you, Mom will.

You're never too sick or ugly for her.

Luke 15 compares God to a woman sweeping the house, frantically in search of a lost coin. She is desperate to find it. The coin in the parable represents the people whom God loves. The story clearly illustrates what British philosopher and author G. K. Chesterton calls "the furious love of God."

The next story in Luke 15 is about a father who wouldn't let go of his son. What a powerful parable! And yet it could have been told of a mother welcoming her child back. Mothers of prodigal children never stop calling, praying, waiting. Even this week I heard a mother say hopefully about her son, "He'll be back."

When no one else will receive you,
Mom will.

What would the parable of the prodigal son sound like if the imagery was feminine instead of masculine? Perhaps it would be like the poignant Brazilian story told by Max Lucado in *No Wonder They Call Him the Savior*.

A beautiful young woman named Christina left her mother, Maria, to try her luck in the big city. But with mere survival much more difficult than she had imagined, Christina turned to prostitution to put food in her stomach and a roof over her head.

The effects of hard living and sin quickly began to take their toll on Christina's beautiful body and disposition. She became lonely and depressed, wanting more than anything to return to her mother and their tiny village. But how could she? As Thomas Wolfe said, "You can't go home again." So her life of misery continued.

But Maria, after figuring out what her restless daughter had done, scraped together enough money for a bus ticket and headed for the city. She combed the bars and hotels, hoping and searching. In prominent places, she left a picture of herself in hopes that her daughter would see the picture and read the message on the back. Sadly, her money ran out and she had to return to her lonely village.

But one evening as Christina descended the stairs from her room, she saw one of the pictures in the hotel parlor. She grabbed it and ran her fingers over it, as if she were a little girl caressing her mother's soft face. Then she noticed the note on the back—a note which said simply, "I love you. No matter what you have done, please come home." And that's just what she did. Thomas Wolfe was wrong![1]

The parable of Luke 15 might also sound like a heart-rending moment from the play *A Raisin in the Sun* by Lorraine Hansberry. It comes after the son has wasted the insurance money his family received from his father's death. He invested it in a business scheme to try to pull his poor, black Chicago family out of their poverty. But his dream was demolished before it even began when his business partner left town with all the money.

His sister was ready to disown him because part of the money he lost was her portion that was supposed to send her to college. "There is nothing left to love," she declares. But her mother rebukes her:

> There is always something left to love. And if you ain't learned that, you ain't learned nothing. Have you cried for that boy today? I don't mean for yourself and for the family 'cause we lost the money. I mean for him: what he been through and what it done to him. Child, when do you

think is the time to love somebody the most?

_____

Our God is like this mother—
wanting to cradle, longing to
nurture, yearning to protect,
aching to forgive.

_____

When they done good and made things easy for
everybody? Well, then you ain't through learning—because that ain't the time at all. It's when
he's at his lowest and can't believe in hisself
'cause the world done whipped him so! When you
starts measuring somebody, measure him right,
child, measure him right. Make sure you done
taken into account what hills and valleys he come
through before he got to wherever he is.[2]

Our God is like this mother—wanting to cradle,
longing to nurture, yearning to protect, aching to
forgive. Isaiah presents this clearly:

> Can a mother forget the baby at her breast
>   and have no compassion on the child she has
>   borne?
> Though she may forget,
>   I will not forget you!
>   Isaiah 49:15

Mother Hunger

God's love knows no end. It is a maternal love that
knows no limitations.

Just as there is a "father hunger," there is also a
"mother hunger" in the land. And again, satisfaction
of our deepest needs can only be met by this One

described in Scripture as "like a mother."

Judith Mattison's poem "What I Need Is a Mother" begins with the desire for a mom:

"What I need is a mother."
The teenage girl, poring over a rack of clothes
at the store, said the words.
But I had been thinking them for days,
"What I need is my mother."
I wanted someone to comfort me
to advise me
to tell me it's all right
to say I love you
to take my problems and solve them for me.

But then her poem flows into prayer as she remembers that the only one who can care for her entirely is the Divine One:

And help me to sense
the tenor of our relationship, Jesus—
yours and mine:
that you are my comfort and my confidant,
that you accept me and help me,
that in a tenderness
which surpasses a mother's love,
you love me.
Thank you, Lord.[3]

Measuring Up

Many have never felt the comfort of intimate, protective relationships with loving mothers. Maybe their mothers were cold and distant, suffered from depression, were cruelly abusive, or maybe were completely absent. But even good mothers can't be perfect and fill all our needs. Only God can do that.

When we turn our longings for a mother relationship from human women, who can never measure up, to a loving God, who is perfect and loving and draws us to his bosom to comfort us, we can finally experience that unconditional, nurturing love we've been yearning for.

Remembering the One Who Gave Us Birth

Some of the saddest words of Scripture creep out of Deuteronomy 32:18: "You forgot the God who gave you birth."

May we never forget God! May we remember how God carried us, gave us birth, nursed us to health, and continues to love us with a perfect mother's love. May we, like Judith Mattison, thank the one who gives us life. May we spend the rest of our lives saying thank you.

Notes:

1. Max Lucado, *No Wonder They Call Him the Savior* (Portland: Multnomah, 1990).

2. Lorraine Hansberry, *A Raisin in the Sun* (New York: Random House, 1969). Used by permission.

3. Judith Mattison, *Prayers from a Mother's Heart* (Minneapolis: Augsburg Fortress Publishing House, 1972). Used by permission.

Focusing Your Faith

1. In what ways was your own mother like God? In what ways was she not?

2. How has your relationship with your mother influenced your mental portrait of God?

3. How do you react emotionally to the idea that God has motherly traits? Had you ever considered that comparison before?

4. Read the story of the prodigal son (Luke 15). How do you think the story would change if Luke had focused on the boy's mother instead of his father?

5. Recall a time in your life when God cared for you in a maternal way?

6. How do you think your relationships might change if you were consistently loving, forgiving, and accepting of others? Ask God to help you become more compassionate and loving towards someone you've had trouble relating to recently.

7. What can we do as Christians to help relieve the "mother hunger" in our church and in our community? How did God use others to show you his maternal nature?

Chapter 4

One Holy Hunger:

Longing for More
in My Marriage

A church where I preached for seven years was unique in that over half of those who attended were between eighteen and twenty-two. That statistic translated into many weddings every May—so many, in fact,

Discovery:

Only God is the perfect mate.

that students would come in September to reserve a date for the peak season. Some hadn't even found a potential spouse yet, but they knew the Lord would provide!

Having participated in a number of weddings, I've learned that the elaborate weddings and receptions many have dreamed of are often quite different from the everyday ceremonies they end up with. Young brides dream that their weddings will be like Maria's in *The Sound of Music* where everything is

47

breathtakingly perfect.

The weddings I've performed never seem to go quite that smoothly, however. A candle goes out; the tenor goes flat; an usher forgets one of the grandmothers; an impatient, overheated ring bearer begins peeling off his clothes. (Fortunately, however, he's unable to decipher the mystery of cuff links!)

The bridesmaids and groomsmen are frozen with embarrassment. The groom can't decide how much to smile: too little looks like he thinks he's making a mistake and too much looks like his mind is on later events!

There is a sense in which "single Christian" is a contradiction in terms, for all Christians are married to God.

The bride's mother is sniffling on the front row. (Someone once said that girls tend to marry men like their fathers, and that's why their mothers cry at the wedding.)

But no matter how many things go wrong at the wedding, it is still an unforgettable moment. The wedding march evokes more powerful emotions than perhaps any other song. It marks the uniting of two lovers—eagerly pledging their lives for love and their love for life.

What a potent picture it is of God's love for us, then, that he is described in Scripture as our spouse. There is a sense in which "single Christian" is a contradiction in terms, for all Christians are married to God. We have offered him the ultimate allegiance of our lives in response to his unremitting love.

This wonderful portrait of God focuses our vision on his unrestrained love, his jealousy, and his incredible grace.

Unrestrained Love

When we think of a bride, we picture a society-page look: exquisite white dress, jewelry, flowers, and innocent smile. "There's no such thing as an ugly bride," an old saying claims.

That's the part of this metaphor where our experience is quite different from God's experience. For God found his people—his bride—abandoned in an open field. What a place to find a wife! And what a condition to find her in!

To emphasize the unconditional nature of God's love, he reminds his people:

> On the day you were born your cord was not cut, nor were you washed with water to make you clean, nor were you rubbed with salt or wrapped in cloths. No one looked on you with pity or had compassion enough to do any of these things for you. Rather, you were thrown out into the open field, for on the day you were born you were despised (Ezekiel 16:4, 5).

God attached his love to his people because of his gracious choosing. The attraction came from his loving nature, not from the inherent loveliness of his bride-to-be.

> Then I passed by and saw you kicking about in your blood, and as you lay there in your blood I said to you, "Live!" I made you grow like a plant of the field. You grew up and developed and became the most beautiful of jewels. Your breasts

were formed and your hair grew, you who were naked and bare (Ezekiel 16:6, 7).

We'll never relate properly to our God until we catch a glimpse of this staggering grace. "While we were still sinners," Paul wrote, "Christ died for us" (Romans 5:8).

We'll never relate properly to our God until we catch a glimpse of this staggering grace.

If we chose a wedding song for the marriage depicted in Ezekiel 16, we couldn't use "Faithful and True." The choir's songs as the bride strolled down the middle aisle would have to be like these:

> Just as I am! poor, wretched, blind
> Sight, riches, healing of the mind,
> Yea, all I need, in Thee to find. . . .

> Nothing in my hand I bring:
> Simply to Thy cross I cling;
> Naked, come to Thee for dress;
> Helpless, look to Thee for grace.

> Amazing grace! how sweet the sound!
> That saved a wretch like me!
> I once was lost, but now am found;
> Was blind, but now I see.

Amazing, indeed! God is like a young man pursuing the love of his life—wearing his best jeans, shaving every week (whether he needs to or not), and calling just to hear her voice on the phone. It is a picture of extravagant, wild, self-abandoned grace:

I clothed you with an embroidered dress and put leather sandals on you. I dressed you in fine linen and covered you with costly garments. I adorned you with jewelry: I put bracelets on your arms and a necklace around your neck, and I put a ring on your nose, earrings on your ears and a beautiful crown on your head. . . . You became very beautiful and rose to be a queen. And your fame spread among the nations on account of your beauty, because the splendor I had given you made your beauty perfect (Ezekiel 16:10-14).

Again, we begin to comprehend a bit of how much God has invested in us and loves us. He is not just an Unmoved Master who sits in heaven and stares at what he has unleashed. He's not a Buddha with glassy eyes and a glum face. He is the Eternal Lover whose relentless courtship culminated in the incarnation of Jesus. The Lover finally came for his bride.

God is our perfect, caring spouse.

God is our perfect, caring spouse. He is the One, the only One, who can fill our deepest needs.

Jealous Love

We've all been warned about the danger of jealousy. We've seen the child who prays for a baby sister—a live toy who can be played with and then put back into the toy box. But then when the baby arrives and is treated like the vice president of the universe, demanding constant attention, there's trouble. Jealousy surfaces.

So perhaps we're surprised to hear Scripture say

that our God is a jealous God. How can that be?

Ezekiel 16 may have the answer: In a monogamous relationship like marriage, complete with its covenant and vow, jealousy is entirely appropriate. In fact, without it there could not be true love. We promise to be exclusively faithful to each other until death, and any breach of that promise would appropriately summon righteous jealousy.

Perhaps you remember the old song "Torn Between Two Lovers" in which a woman tries to comfort her husband and justify to him her reasons for having an extra-marital affair:

> There's been another man that I've needed and
> I've loved.
> But that doesn't mean I love you less.
>
> And he knows he can't possess me and he knows
> he never will.
> There's just this empty place inside of me that
> only he can fill.
>
> Torn between two lovers, feelin' like a fool.
> Lovin' both of you is breaking all the rules.
>
> You mustn't think you failed me just because
> there's someone else;
> You were the first real love I ever had and all the
> things I ever said,
> I swear they still are true.
> For no one else can have the part of me I gave to
> you.
>
> Torn between two lovers, feelin' like a fool.
> Lovin' both of you is breaking all the rules.[1]

Asking someone not to be hurt or upset about broken promises and vows is crazy. Adultery always brings deep pain. It is accompanied by deceit, betrayal, and loss of self-respect. It ruins relationships that are built on trust and founded on commitment.

God's love is an exclusive love. It permits no rivals.

This is the gut-wrenching jealousy that God experiences when his bride breaks faith. He painfully chokes out his grief over his people's waywardness:

> But you trusted in your beauty and used your fame to become a prostitute. You lavished your favors on anyone who passed by and your beauty became his. . . . You adulterous wife! You prefer strangers to your own husband! Every prostitute receives a fee, but you give gifts to all your lovers, bribing them to come to you from everywhere for your illicit favors. So in your prostitution you are the opposite of others; no one runs after you for your favors. You are the very opposite, for you give payment and none is given to you (Ezekiel 16:15, 32-34).

God's people of Judah failed to give all their love to their Lord. Rather, they shared their love with the other gods of the land. They eagerly participated in the idolatry of the people around them. And in that participation they broke their marriage vows with God. They neglected the very first commandment: "I am the LORD your God, who brought you out of Egypt, out of the land of slavery. You shall have no other gods before me" (Exodus 20:2, 3).

God's love is an exclusive love. It permits no

rivals. God refuses to be replaced in our hearts by someone or something that catches our attention. He will not share the supreme place in our lives. Only God can receive our ultimate devotion, energy, and trust.

We must turn our eyes from the alluring entice-ments of the fatal attractions around us. Some are drawn by a quest for knowledge, others by wealth, some by sex, others by "good causes," some by alle-giance to country, and others by a career. Rather than permit us to keep a lover on the side, God regretfully allows us to leave him for our lover—as when Jesus sorrowfully watched a rich young ruler walk away because he wouldn't give up his pursuit of wealth (Luke 18:18-30).

James picks up this powerful theme of God's jealousy when he reprimands Christians for their unhealthy love for the things of this world: "You adulterous people, don't you know that friendship with the world is hatred toward God? Anyone who chooses to be a friend of the world becomes an enemy of God" (James 4:4). Then in verse 5 he gives the reason: "God *yearns jealously* for the spirit that he has made to dwell in us" (NRSV).

Incredible Grace

Because the people of Judah violated their agree-ment with the Lord, it seems like they would be forever banished from his house.

I will sentence you to the punishment of women who commit adultery and who shed blood; I will bring upon you the blood vengeance of my wrath and jealous anger. Then I will hand you over to your lovers, and they will tear down your mounds

and destroy your lofty shrines. They will strip you
of your clothes and take your fine jewelry and
leave you naked and bare. They will bring a mob
against you, who will stone you and hack you to
pieces with their swords (Ezekiel 16:38-40).

These aren't exactly words of hope! Could it be
that people of God who are caught in the very act of
adultery will be stoned to death? Is there no second
chance?

*God, the Divine Lover, would recon-
cile people to himself through this
extravagant gift.*

Incredible news of grace returns in verses 59-63.
Since Judah had been unwilling to keep the covenant, God says that out of his own deep reservoir of
love he will draw waters of renewal. He would
establish an everlasting covenant.
But how is that possible? How could we ever
deserve that? We can't! Look at God's next words: "I
make atonement for you for all you have done. . . ."
God would make it possible by atoning—words that
ultimately lead us to the sacrifice of God's son, Jesus
Christ, on the cross. God, the Divine Lover, would
reconcile people to himself through this extravagant
gift. He would offer his Son as a substitute for us,
allowing Jesus to bear the consequences for our sins.
This helps us understand Paul's never-ending
gratitude for being "in Christ." For "in [Christ] we
have redemption through his blood, the forgiveness
of sins, in accordance with the riches of God's grace
that he lavished on us with all wisdom and understanding" (Ephesians 1:7, 8). He never forgot the

Lord he'd met on the road to Damascus. And he
never quit reflecting on his baptism into Jesus
Christ.

Wedding Vows

Baptism is a beautiful wedding ceremony: an
event that marks our entrance into God's family.
But every day for Christians means living out the
vows of baptism. Through Communion we promise
again to love, honor, and cherish God and be God's
alone. As I regularly commune with God, I recommit
my love in these vows:

> I again commit my life to you, O God of Love,
>   promising to follow you—faithful to the end.
> May my mind be captured by your sufficiency;
> May my heart be filled with your love;
> May my hands be lifted to your praise;
> May my knees be bowed to your majesty;
> May my life be transformed into your likeness;
> May my vows be faithfully kept forever!

_____

Notes

1. Phillip Jarrell and Peter Yarrow, "Torn Between Two
Lovers," p c 1976 Muscle Shoals Sound Pub. Co. and Silver
Dawn Music. International copyright secured. All rights
reserved. Used by permission.

Focusing Your Faith

1. What could the Lord have seen so appealing in us that would cause him to make us his bride?

2. What is the worst thing about loneliness? What is the best thing to do to overcome that overwhelming feeling? How can you help someone else who is struggling with loneliness?

3. Have you ever been betrayed by your partner in a relationship? Have you ever betrayed your partner? How do you think God feels when we betray him or, simply, stop loving him?

4. Have you ever found yourself in a relationship in which you asked, "If God is all-powerful, all-knowing, and all-loving, why doesn't he do something to help me?" What was the outcome?

5. Why do you think a close relationship with a life-partner—a spouse—is so important to us?

6. If baptism is like a wedding ceremony with the Lord, what is the significance of the vows we make with him? What could you do to celebrate your anniversaries?

7. What has God done for you or given you that shows he is a perfect, caring spouse?

Chapter 5

One Holy Hunger:

Seeking

Security and Safety

W hat passage of Scripture is better known or more loved than Psalm 23? Many of us could quote it before we could actually read it. "No single psalm," Bernhard Anderson has written, "has expressed more powerfully man's prayer of confidence 'out of the depths' to the God whose purpose alone gives meaning to the span of life, from womb to tomb."

> **Discovery:**
>
> *The Lord is my search-and-rescue Shepherd.*

It is a poem which children recite, which sustains the mature when life becomes complicated, and which becomes a peaceful benediction on the lips of the dying. It's a statement of faith that I've recited over a large casket containing the body of a much-loved elder and over a tiny casket holding a 21-inch baby.

But sometimes Scriptures that are so well known are not known so well! It might help to hear a fresh translation of the psalm by prolific religious writer Bernhard Anderson:

Yahweh is my Shepherd, nothing do I lack.
   In grassy meadows he makes me repose,
   By quiet waters he leads me.
   He revives my whole being!
   He guides me into the right paths, for the
      honor of his Name.
Even when I go through the valley of deep
      darkness,
   I fear nothing sinister;
   for You are at my side!
   Your rod and staff reassure me.

You spread out before me a table,
   in sight of those who threaten me.
   You pour upon my head festive oil.
   My cup is brimming over!
Certainly, divine goodness and grace attend me
      throughout all my days,
   and I shall be a guest in Yahweh's house
      as long as I live.[1]

The Shepherd's Sheep

To appreciate what this picture of God teaches us about him, we must first catch what it implies about us, his sheep. In a church where I ministered, a woman wrote the church leaders asking them to quit referring to the people as sheep. She didn't think it was very flattering. That's an understatement!

Sheep are not smart animals. Have you ever been to the circus and seen a trained sheep? Probably not!

Unlike some animals, sheep have very little sense of tracking. If they become lost, they don't find their way home very easily. Oh, I know:

Little Bo Peep has lost her sheep
and doesn't know where to find them.
Leave them alone and they'll come home,
wagging their tails behind them.

But you have to watch out for false doctrine in nursery rhymes! Little Bo Peep can wait and wait all she wants, but eventually she's going to have to go find those sheep. Isaiah's words are a bit more accurate: "We all, like sheep, have gone astray" (53:6). Sheep are basically clueless animals, with no idea where they came from or where they're going. Sound familiar?

Sheep are not powerful animals. When was the last time you saw a sign reading "BEWARE OF SHEEP"? When I ran in the New York City Marathon, we went through all five boroughs of the city. Several sections were filled with graffiti from street gangs. Some had adopted the names of animals: "Jaguars rule"; "Wolves rule"; "Pythons rule." But I never saw one that said, "Sheep rule." That's not exactly the image a tough street gang wants to portray!

Sheep are defenseless animals. They have no sharp hooves, claws, or teeth. They're not fast like deer. Nor do they have shells like turtles. Without a shepherd, they're at the mercy of any coyote, mountain lion, bear, or thief that comes along.

Sheep are not clean animals. Again, I can hear someone ready to quote a nursery rhyme to me: "Mary had a little lamb, its fleece was white as snow." Again, don't believe everything you hear!

Mother Goose must have visited a petting zoo.
Unlike other animals, sheep prefer to stay dirty.
They are more piggish than pigs.

Now do you see why this woman didn't think it
was very flattering to be called sheep? And yet how
insightfully the Bible describes us: people who tend
to get lost; people who can't defend themselves; and
people who desperately need a good cleaning! We,
like sheep, must depend totally on our Shepherd for
survival.

A Message of Warning

The popularity of horoscopes, astrology, cults,
and new-age gurus testify to the fact that many
today have lost their direction and want someone to
make their decisions for them, take care of them,
and protect them. That's why Jim Bakker and cult
leaders Jim Jones, David Koresh, and hundreds of
others like them have had such a following. Many of
these earthly guides have tried to take the place of
God and have led their followers down the wrong
path.

A Message of Comfort

God, too, knows we have a need for shepherds on
earth. That's why he encourages the church to
provide them for its flocks. These experienced, wise
souls can offer the leadership, support, and guidance
we need to make us a unified body in Christ. But,
while God-sanctioned, these shepherds are not
perfect. They make mistakes and sometimes disap-
point us. That's why we continually listen to the
heavenly Shepherd's call to follow him above all. He
will never let us down.

The presence of our Shepherd brings great comfort to us. He is the one who gives us rest, water, food, and protection. His presence means everything to us. That doesn't mean we won't have enemies or we won't have to pass through dark valleys; rather, it promises that he will be with us wherever we go. The writer of Psalm 23 knows that evil is present. But evil isn't feared, for we have confidence in God. No wonder we find this psalm in so many hospital rooms and printed on the programs at funerals. The comforting promise in Scripture isn't that we will be protected from disappointment and pain; rather, it is that the Lord is a shepherd who will never abandon us.

> He tends his flock like a shepherd:
> He gathers the lambs in his arms
> and carries them close to his heart;
> he gently leads those that have young.
> Isaiah 40:11

A Message of Guidance

Like sheep we long for and need a shepherd who can lead us beside quiet waters (Psalm 23:2), a shepherd who will guide us in the right paths (v. 3). This is the guidance we are offered by the Maker of the universe. He leads us in the "paths of righteousness."

Of course, many resent this intrusion into their lives. They want to find their own way, they say. They don't need anyone's help. And yet at one time or another they get a nagging sense that maybe they really are lost. Maybe they didn't find all they intended to find in life.

Those who have made the decision to follow the

Good Shepherd, Jesus Christ, the one who laid down his life for his sheep, have learned to welcome his guidance as a gift of love and concern rather than as an unwelcomed intrusion. They are thankful for a God who not only made them but who shows them how to live an abundant life (John 10:10). They've learned to sing with great joy:

> He leadeth me: O blessed tho't!
> O words with heav'nly comfort fraught!
> Whate'er I do, where'er I be,
> Still 'tis God's hand that leadeth me.

A Message of Sufficiency

A little girl, when asked to recite the beginning of Psalm 23 in Sunday school, said boldly, "The Lord is my Shepherd; that's all I want." That's not quite how it reads, but that's a wonderful interpretation of what it means!

Most people recite this verse without giving a thought to what it really says. When I speak the words of Psalm 23, I'm saying that I am content in whatever my situation is—because the Lord is with me. Perhaps it was in the back of Paul's mind when he wrote to the Philippians:

> I have learned to be content whatever the circum-
> stances. I know what it is to be in need, and I
> know what it is to have plenty. I have learned the
> secret of being content in any and every situation,
> whether well fed or hungry, whether living in
> plenty or in want. I can do everything through
> him who gives me strength (Philippians 4:11b-13).

Do we really believe that? Do we honestly believe that we need nothing else as long as we know that the Lord is our shepherd? Could we say with the psalmist, "Whom have I in heaven but you? And earth has nothing I desire besides you" (Psalm 73:25)?

God is the One who can fill our lives
for eternity!

Our whole culture screams at us that we are lacking something. It pleads with us to invest in one more product or take one more trip so that we can be happy.

But in stark contrast, the biblical view is that God is our ultimate need. All the thrills around us can satisfy us only for a passing moment. God is the One who can fill our lives for eternity! As the French monk Thomas Merton put it in his last public address before his death: "That is his call to us—simply to be people who are content to live close to him and to renew the kind of life in which the closeness is felt and experienced."

The Searching Shepherd

One final note about this Shepherd: he is diligently looking for you. No matter how faithful or faithless you might have been, he's searching. No matter how "together" your life might be or how broken, he's tracking you. He pursues you constantly to bring you to salvation. And, once he has you, no one can steal you from him (John 10:28, 29).

Do you remember Jesus' parable—the one that almost gets overlooked because it's in the shadow of the Prodigal Son?

Suppose one of you has a hundred sheep and

loses one of them. Does he not leave the ninety-nine in the open country and go after the lost sheep until he finds it? And when he finds it, he joyfully puts it on his shoulders and goes home. Then he calls his friends and neighbors together and says, "Rejoice with me; I have found my lost sheep" (Luke 15:4-6).

Again, we are drawn back to the "scandalous" love of God. How dare the shepherd leave the ninety-nine for just one lost sheep! An old gospel hymn diminishes the scandal a bit as it begins: "There were ninety and nine that safely lay in the shelter of the fold." That's a beautiful picture—but not the one Jesus painted. In his story, the shepherd didn't leave his sheep in the shelter of the fold; he left them out in the open country and went out after the one that was lost.

Why? Why would he do that? You know, don't you? You know why he left the ninety-nine to look for the one.

Because it was you who was tired and thirsty and hungry! It was you who crouched, bleating helplessly on the narrow ledge above the bottomless abyss! It was you who felt, beyond all hope, the strong, sure grip of this search-and-rescue Shepherd, the One who loves you with such deep, intense love!

Notes

1. Bernhard Anderson, *Out of the Depths* (Philadelphia: Westminster Press, 1974). Used by permission.

Focusing Your Faith

1. Which passage of scripture brings you the most comfort when you are truly troubled?

2. After reviewing the characteristics of sheep, tell what traits you most identify with. How are you different from sheep?

3. How do you think of yourself—as the one lost lamb that the Shepherd went after, or one of the ninety-nine that he left in the field? Why?

4. What person do you most consider your shepherd? How has he/she helped guide you?

5. When you first came to know God, had you been looking for him, or did he come looking for you?

6. How does it make you feel to know that you have a search-and-rescue God who relentlessly pursues you?

7. Recall a time in your life when you realized God was rescuing you. How did you react to him?

PART 2:

WE'RE STARVING TO DEATH FROM FALSE IDEAS ABOUT GOD

Chapter 6

False Idea:

God
Wants Me to Be
Afraid of Him

So many of the biblical pictures of God point us to his nearness. He is a personal God who comes to dwell among us. Though it is difficult for adults to believe that he could really be near us, children apparently don't

> **Discovery:**
>
> *God wants me to know him personally and to love him.*

have that problem. A couple of books have published letters children were asked to write to God. They are filled with confidence that God is involved in our lives and that he's an approachable God:

> Dear God, Thank you for my baby brother but what I prayed for was a puppy. Joyce

> Dear God, I would like to know why all the things you said are in red? Joanne

Dear God, Maybe Cain and Abel would not kill
each [other] so much if they had their own rooms.
It works with my brother. Larry.[1]

Dear God, Why do so many persons who begin
with "I" fight in wars. Iranians. Iracs. Israel.
Indians. You name it. Is it just an accident?
Maybe you should check on it. It gives all the "I"
people a bad name! Best wishes, Ingred.

Special delivery to God, Why not have a few new
commandments. How about one that goes—Thou
should not have to wash dishes until you are big
and older and have a family or two of your own.
Think about this, Stephanie.[2]

Oh, that we could have the boldness to come before
God like these children, understanding that he is
One who has chosen to be among us!

A Glimpse of God

But while Scripture describes God as a personal
being, it also portrays him as one who is completely
sovereign. He is a transcendent God, a being beyond
comprehension, who is not made in our image.

Right after describing the confidence we can have
in drawing near to God, the writer of Hebrews
reminds us: "It is a dreadful thing to fall into the
hands of the living God" (10:31). Later he admon-
ishes Christians to "worship God acceptably with
reverence and awe, for our 'God is a consuming fire' "
(12:28, 29).

We must beware of focusing solely on the biblical
pictures of God that lead us to believe that he is just
like us—only a little larger and more powerful.

Although God is approachable, he is not just an extra-strong big brother. He is *God*, and we should be filled with wonder that we can approach him.

Imagine what it might be like for a slug to contemplate a human being. You have to figure there are a few subtleties the slug doesn't quite catch. That's undoubtedly something like what happens when humans contemplate God. We can only begin to grasp faint notions of his power, love, and holiness.

---

*We can only begin to grasp
faint notions of his power, love,
and holiness.*

Though we might want to see him more clearly, we should be forewarned that, without exception, those in the Bible who glimpsed the holiness of God were dumbstruck and terrified.

- ❖ Job, after hearing from the Lord, cried: "I am unworthy—how can I reply to you? . . . My ears had heard of you but now my eyes have seen you. Therefore I despise myself and repent in dust and ashes" (Job 40:4; 42:5, 6).

- ❖ Habakkuk, after entering the watchtower and waiting for God's answer, was seized by dread: "I heard and my heart pounded, my lips quivered at the sound; decay crept into my bones, and my legs trembled" (Habakkuk 3:16).

- ❖ Peter, recognizing the glory of God in the

works of Jesus, responds: "Go away from
me, Lord; I am a sinful man!" (Luke 5:8).

❖ John, having received a revelation of
Christ's glory, "fell at his feet as though
dead" (Revelation 1:17).

We have many adjectives that describe this "other-
ness" of God: "transcendent," "sovereign," "awesome," "mysterious." But the word Scripture uses
most often is "holy."

In several Old Testament books, God is called
"the Holy One of Israel." Most of the occurrences of
the phrase, however, are in Isaiah. And is it any
wonder? This prophet could never forget a startling
vision he had in 742 B.C.—a vision in which he
caught a glimpse of God's awesomeness.

The Vision of Isaiah

The vision came "in the year that King Uzziah
died" (Isaiah 6:1). This was a time of national tragedy, for Uzziah had been king of Judah for fifty-two
years. (Imagine having a president who's been in
office since the 1940s!) The king had been basically
good, but had been struck by God with leprosy in his
older years for falling into the pit of pride.

Though the king is dead, Isaiah enters the temple
and sees another King—the One who sits on the
heavenly throne. He is "high and exalted, and the
train of his robe filled the temple." Above the King
hover angelic beings called seraphs. In Egypt the
seraphs would watch over the king to protect him.
But in Isaiah's vision they have to use four of their
six wings to protect themselves. God doesn't need
protection from anyone.

Note carefully what the heavenly seraphs are

calling out to one another:

Holy, holy, holy is the LORD Almighty;
the whole earth is full of his glory (v. 3a).

"Holy, holy, holy" is a Hebrew expression for our
word "holiest." There is no one to whom God can be
compared. To complete the scene of mystery and
majesty, Isaiah adds that "the doorposts and thresh-
olds shook and the temple was filled with smoke"
(v. 4).

Immediately the prophet saw himself as ruined.
"Woe to me!" he cried out. In the presence of God he
could see his own impurity more than ever before.
Only when a coal was taken from the altar and used
to purge his lips was he able to stand and respond to
God's call to service.

John's Vision

We can hear echoes of this vision in the New
Testament when John describes his encounter with
God's throne room:

In the center, around the throne, were four living
creatures, and they were covered with eyes, in
front and in back. The first living creature was
like a lion, the second was like an ox, the third
had a face like a man, the fourth was like a flying
eagle. Each of the four living creatures had six
wings and was covered with eyes all around, even
under his wings. Day and night they never stop
saying:

Holy, holy, holy
is the Lord God Almighty,
who was, and is, and is to come.
Revelation 4:6b-8

What Is Holiness?

There are at least two aspects to the concept of God's holiness.

1. Separation. When Scripture speaks of a "holy day" it means a day that is set apart or specially designated for some purpose. Jerusalem is called a "holy hill" because it was separated from other cities to become the place of God's temple.

God's holiness implies that he is separate from us. "I am God, and not man—the Holy One among you" (Hosea 11:9b). If you're talking about personality, we are more like God than we are like a cricket. But if you're speaking about infinity, we are more like the cricket than like God. He is a wholly supreme being, the essence of holiness. His ways are mysterious and can never be fully explored from our shallow perspective.

He is a wholly supreme being, the essence of holiness.

God is not just a kind Grandfather-in-Heaven. He isn't a cosmic Mr. Rogers. Even when God chooses to draw near to us there is still a clear line of distinction. That's why Jesus' claim to be God ("Before Abraham was born, I am!" John 8:58) was so scandalous. In fact, it was that claim that killed him.

German theologian Rudolph Otto says holiness refers to an "awful mystery." We are both drawn to and repelled by that which is holy. We desire both to run to the God who loves us and to run from the Presence that convicts us. With Peter we cry, "Go away from me, Lord; I am a sinful person!" (Luke 5:8).

2. Absolute purity. In God there is no hint of
iniquity, not a drop of evil. He cannot lie. Sin is a
problem that infects humanity; it does not infect
God.

Living Grace

At times we don't see our sinfulness because we
aren't looking at God. Rather, we're looking at all
the people around us. Then we deceive ourselves into
thinking that we're not really that bad, after all.

Our imaginary scale has a moral continuum with
Adolf Hitler at 1 and the apostle Paul at 10. On that
scale, we might picture ourselves much closer to the
10 than the 1. But a better scale, the one that Isaiah
discovered, would put Hitler at 1 and God at 10. On
this continuum, we're much closer to the 1 than the
10!

"Men are never duly touched and impressed with
a conviction of their insignificance," John Calvin,
sixteenth century church reformer, wrote, "until
they have contrasted themselves with the majesty of
God." The more we look at God, the more evil we
discover within us. No wonder Isaiah exclaimed,
"Woe to me!"

*Those who are hungering for God
never take sin lightly.*

Those who are hungering for God never take sin
lightly. They never tolerate it or make excuses for it.
They understand that sin is cosmic treason. It is
spitting in the face of a holy God. They no longer
wonder how God could deal so severely with Ananias
and Sapphira (Acts 5); they now wonder how he can

keep from dealing similarly with all of us.

The only way we can live in God's presence is by
his own sovereign grace. Isaiah was a broken man
whom God restored. God chose to take a man with a
dirty mouth and make him into his own spokesman.

> Then one of the seraphs flew to me with a live coal
> in his hand, which he had taken with tongs from
> the altar. With it he touched my mouth and said,
> "See, this has touched your lips; your guilt is taken
> away and your sin atoned for" (Isaiah 6:6, 7).

Perhaps in this text we get a peek at God's atoning work at Calvary. People are separated from God
because of sin. Because of his perfect holiness, God
can't just wink at our sins. A perfect sacrifice had to
be made. And since we can't make it because of our
sins, God came himself in Jesus Christ to become the
sacrifice. (See Romans 3:25, 26.)

Let Me Be Like You, God

After Isaiah's guilt was removed, he heard the
voice of the Lord asking, "Whom shall I send? And
who will go for us?" The prophet responded, "Here
am I. Send me!" (6:8).

How could we do anything less? The Holy One
deserves our lives. Through the sacrifice of his Son,
he has graciously declared us to be "saints," holy
people. Now we should offer him our lives completely
so that he can free us more and more from sin. "For
God did not call us to be impure," Paul reminds us,
"but to live a holy life" (1 Thessalonians 4:7).

Remember—the goal of this book isn't to produce
more data. In other words, we don't just want to add
the word "holiness" to our list of Qualities of God.

Rather, our recognition that the God who longs

for us is holy should drive us to our knees, begging him to make us more like him. We want to treat people the way God does; we want to live with values that are the same as his; we want to have attitudes that are godly; we want our actions to be pure. We want to become like God our Father, our Mother, our Spouse, and our Shepherd.

Notes:

1. Stuart Hample and Eric Marshall, compilers, *Children's Letters to God* (New York: Workman Publishing, 1991).

2. David Heller, *Dear God, What Religion Were the Dinosaurs?: More Children's Letters to God* (New York: Bantam Books, 1990).

Focusing Your Faith

1. Write a letter to your friend, God.

2. Describe an experience you've had in which you witnessed firsthand the awesome majesty of God.

3. What frightens you most about the power of God? What comforts you most about the power of God?

4. Why is it difficult for us to feel as close to God as children do?

5. Why do people like to think of God as an extension of themselves?

6. As a teenager, what was your mental picture of God? How has that image of God influenced your life choices?

7. Would you say that you have responded to God most of your life out of love, out of fear, or out of duty? Why? How has your view of God changed since you were younger?

Chapter 7

False Idea:

God
Is Going to
Zap Me

Woody Allen's film, *Crimes and Misdemeanors,* centers on a modern Jewish physician named Judah whose adultery has caught up with him and is starting to cause his life to unravel. In the midst of his turmoil, Judah seeks to return to his biblical roots. Specifically, he wants to know, "What does God think of me?"

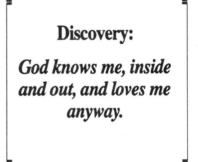

Discovery:

God knows me, inside and out, and loves me anyway.

Unfortunately, the only picture of God that had made much of an impression on him from his synagogue-attending days was the All-Seeing Eye.

This mammoth eyeball had been a dominant image in his life. Every time he thought of God he thought of the eye. Whenever he made decisions he remembered it. He even became an ophthalmologist!

I remember similarly being impressed by the

awesome image of this huge eyeball hovering over my every act. The fear skyrocketed every time we sang:

There's an Eye watching you.
Watching you, watching you,
Every day mind the course you pursue;
Watching you, watching you,
There's an all-seeing Eye watching you.

It isn't unusual to hear someone complain, "No one really knows me." They're decrying the shallowness of many of our human relationships. When someone asks how we're doing, we understand that the socially acceptable answer is "fine." You may really be thinking, "The kids have been driving me crazy, and I nearly boiled them for breakfast," but you still say, "fine." And you smile.

No Secrets

We think we'd love having someone who understands us fully. But are we sure? Can you imagine having someone who really does see you fully? Such a person might have access to every thought, every action, and every mistake in your life. Imagine not having *anything* secret!

He is an All-Seeing Eye watching us.

And yet that's just what Psalm 139 is telling us about God—he knows more than we'd care to have known if given the choice. He is an All-Seeing Eye watching us. He sees every nook and cranny of my life: every broken window, every piece of mildewed carpet, every chipped tile, every inch of flaking trim.

Everything is subject to his scrutiny:

> O LORD, you have searched me
>   and you know me.
> You know when I sit and when I rise;
>   you perceive my thoughts from afar.
> You discern my going out and my
>   lying down;
>   you are familiar with all my ways.
> Before a word is on my tongue
>   you know it completely, O LORD.
> You hem me in—behind and before;
>   you have laid your hand upon me.
> Such knowledge is too wonderful for
>   me,
>   too lofty for me to attain.
>   Psalm 139:1-6

I remember being frightened by this psalm.
Where is the grace in it? Doesn't it just tell us of a
God who sees everything? A first-rate snoop? I
pictured a huge eyeball that was swollen from anger
and streaked with red from squinting.

An Insider's Look

Omniscience is too cold a word to describe the
first six verses of this psalm. It isn't speaking gener-
ally about how knowledgeable God is. The point isn't
that God is a bright, cosmic Rhodes scholar who
knows the answers to the mysteries of history and
the riddles of the universe. Scripture does tell us
that God is all-knowing (see Job 38, 39) but that isn't
the focus of this psalm.

Rather, David says that God knows *me*. In my
desire to know God, I must remember that his
knowledge of me is prevenient—he knows me before

I know him!

David describes six ways that God has shown an intimate knowledge of him in Psalm 139:

1. God has *searched* me (v. 1). The Holy Spirit continues to search my heart and soul to know the real me. From his flawless insider's knowledge of me, he's not only able to understand my prayers and groanings, but able to interpret and explain them to God as well (Romans 8:26, 27).

2. God *knows* me (v. 1, 2). It is a special relationship, an intimate understanding of a best friend. And it doesn't matter whether the psalmist is resting ("when I sit") or moving ("when I rise").

3. God *perceives* my thoughts (v. 2). A few years ago, I was frightened by my constant voice problems (not a good problem for a minister to have!), so I visited an ear, nose, and throat specialist. Dr. Hatfield (whose office, I promise, was across the hallway from Dr. McCoy) wanted to look inside my throat with a fiber-optic snake. First, he sprayed my mouth with something he said would taste like bubble gum. I can only assume he gets his gum from the bottom of old church pews—it was rancid!

He guided this fiber-optic serpent up my nose, and the next thing I knew it was headed down my throat. While I concentrated on not gagging, he peered at my vocal folds in action. It's a strange sensation to know that a man standing beside you is watching your insides at work.

David said that God is able to do that. He sees my thoughts from afar. Nothing escapes him.

4. God *discerns* my comings and goings (v. 3). It doesn't matter whether I am on the run or resting, God knows where I am.

5. God is *familiar* with my ways (v. 3). He knows my habits, my weaknesses, and my strengths. He

knows all my business.

6. God *knows my words* before they're on my tongue (v. 4). He knows what I'm going to say before I say it. Have you ever had a friend so close that you can finish sentences for each other? That's a scary part of marriage: after a decade or two you begin to frequently hear your spouse say, "I knew you'd say that." You eventually run out of original material!

One week I had to leave town to speak and forgot to tell either my secretary or my running buddy I was going. When my buddy came by my office to pick me up to run at noon, he asked, "Where's Mike?"

"I don't know," Cecelia replied. "I think he left, but he didn't even write his bulletin article." Leon delightfully (I'm sure) told her he could take care of that. So he sat at my desk with my pen and wrote my bulletin article for the church newsletter.

When I returned later that week and read the bulletin, I thought, "I don't remember writing that . . . but it sounds like me." I told him later, "That was just what I would have written. Sure, I'd have done it lots better, but that's basically what I would have said." We have one of those "before a word is off my tongue" kind of friendships.

The insights described in verses 1-6 are over-whelming—even frightening! God knows everything about me: my strong points, my vulnerable points, my frustrations, my sins. He knows me inside and out and loves me anyway. Nothing escapes the gaze of this All-Seeing Eye.

The Relentless Retina

Is there a way to hide from this penetrating look? Can we, like children, pull blankets over our heads so we will be "safe"? "Where can I go from your

Spirit? / Where can I flee from your presence?" the psalmist asks (v. 7).

Maybe we could try fleeing upward—no, God is in the heavens. How about downward? No, God is present in the depths (*Sheol*) as well. Let's try the east ("the wings of the dawn") or the west ("the far side of the sea" from a Palestinian perspective). Nope, God is there as well.

Possibly we could just wait out the daytime and let the darkness protect us. That won't help either, because God can see in the dark:

> Even the darkness will not be dark to you;
> the night will shine like the day,
> for darkness is as light to you.
> Psalm 139:12

Even in the safest, most hidden place—our mothers' wombs—we are not removed from his presence.

> For you created my inmost being;
> you knit me together in my mother's womb.
> My frame was not hidden from you
> when I was made in the secret place.
> When I was woven together in the depths of the
> earth,
> your eyes saw my unformed body.
> Psalm 139:13, 15

We feel the desire to run, as described by Francis Thompson's poem "The Hound of Heaven," in this thrilling passage: "I fled Him down the nights and down the days; I fled Him, down the arches of the years. . . ." But David discovers that rather than being pursued everywhere, he is awaited: "You are there . . . there . . . even there."

This level of intimate knowledge is too much to

comprehend. Actually, it's enough to scare us to death! For where is the word of grace in this psalm? Where is the message to protect us from this relentless retina?

A Wink of Approval

The word of grace comes, I think, at the very end of the psalm. The last two verses set the context—a context of security and acceptance.

Search me, O God, and know my heart;
    test me and know my anxious thoughts.
See if there is any offensive way in me,
    and lead me in the way everlasting.
                              Psalm 139:23, 24

Why would the psalmist invite God to continue searching? Isn't that like asking the IRS to check not only your return from last year but the ones from the previous ten years as well?

One relationship in life has helped me understand why he might welcome God's continuing search. There is one person who knows more about my shortcomings and sins than anyone else. While many friends could write chapters about my goofs, my wife could produce a book. (She might even say a series of books!) And yet she is also the one who loves me the most!

"Search me and know my heart" could be spoken only by someone who feels completely loved and accepted, one whose hunger for God has been satisfied. These words could be spoken only to One who unconditionally loves the person he is watching. He sees every square inch of my life—and still he loves me unconditionally. He knows my successes and my failures; he sees my strengths and my weaknesses;

he understands how holy and unholy I can be. And even though he expects me to continue letting him perform his sacred surgery—cutting out the cancerous cells of my life—he never withholds his love.

If you look at it long enough, you might even see it wink!

God is an all-seeing eye, but not the eye I imagined as a teenager. Psalm 139 describes the caring, constant view of a loving parent or a true friend, not the stinging, oppressive view of a cosmic critic. Instead of being swollen with anger and streaked with red, this eye gleams with a mother's joy and a father's approval.

If you look at it long enough, you might even see it wink!

Focusing Your Faith

1. Choose a song which best describes your view of God today, such as "From a Distance," "There's an Eye Watching You," or "Amazing Grace."

2. How can learning more about God help satisfy your hunger to be understood?

3. Recall a recent experience when you felt the watchful eye of God.

4. How do people today try to escape God's watchful eye? Where do you go to avoid it? Do you feel loved there?

5. To what person on earth could you honestly and comfortably say, "Search me and know my heart"? Why?

6. How many of your friends know the *real* you? How many do you think you'd have if they did really know you?

7. How does it make you feel to hear that God knows the real you, and loves you anyway?

Chapter 8

False Idea:

God Never
Comes Through

It wasn't until my second year of Little League, at the ripe age of eight, that I figured out how to hit a base-ball. It was a great relief to my parents, not because they were embarrassed that I wasn't a Willie Mays at

> ### Discovery:
> *God always keeps his promises.*

age seven, but because I didn't have to spend another summer in frustration. (My mom remembers my first coach teaching me to lean over the plate so I would be hit by the pitch and get walked. Friends have said they think this memory explains a lot about me!)

After realizing his son really could hit a ball, my dad told me he'd give me a buck if I hit a home run. It still looked like a fairly safe bet.

The next game, I bunted my first time up. The

catcher pounced on the ball and did what any Little League catcher would do: he fired it into right field. So on the overthrow I rounded first and headed to second. The right fielder did what any respectable Little League right fielder would do: he zipped it into left field. That's when I took off for third base. Then the left fielder heaved it into the dugout, so I got to trot home.

After the game I asked my dad for the dollar. "But you didn't hit a home run," he objected. Oh yes I did! I started the play at home plate and ended at home plate, having hit the ball one time. In my book, that's called a home run. So he paid.

We eventually have to ask, Is he trustworthy?

After hearing my story, the local newspaper carried an article about my well-rewarded home run. (I was sure at the time this article was unrelated to the fact that my uncle was the editor . . . and my dad was the business manager . . . and my grandfather was the publisher!)

Why did he pay? I wondered years later. After all he was *technically* correct: one bunt plus three errors does not equal a home run. But eventually I knew why he paid a debt he didn't owe. My father loved me and appreciated my effort to meet his challenge. He also knew that if I didn't think I could trust him on that deal, I might not trust him the next time. And a father doesn't want his child to think he isn't trustworthy.

As we continue examining the insights of Scripture about God, we eventually have to ask, Is he trustworthy? There is a clear answer that echoes through the pages: "Your faithfulness reaches to the skies" (Psalm 108:4). But there are times when such statements sound like cheap, chirpy optimism—or like wishful thinking.

Can God Be Trusted?

There are times of crisis when God doesn't seem to be faithful to his promises. For example, haven't you ever frowned doubtfully when reading, "Whatever you ask in prayer you will receive"? Or how about, "Ask and it will be given to you"? Or maybe, "The prayer of the righteous is powerful and effective"?

I know there have been times in my own life when my prayers didn't exactly seem to "avail much." When our daughter showed signs of being developmentally delayed, Diane and I prayed fervently that she would be "all right" (having little idea at the time what that might mean). As we learned that she would have problems and then that she was retarded and years later that she was fighting for her life with a disease, we kept praying. But the thought did cross my mind: Is anyone listening?

You've had a few quiet moments when the same thought inched across your mind, too, haven't you? And if you think that God fudged on one promise, you might find it hard to trust him with other promises.

Here's another one that goes down hard at times: Ask God and he'll give you wisdom (James 1:5). But I think of some godly people I've known who prayed, desperately seeking God's wisdom about whether they should go to the mission field or not. Then after sensing his blessing and after preparing, they could find no financial support. Eventually they gave up their dreams, wondering about all this wisdom they'd been promised.

Another promise that Christians have heard for nearly two thousand years now is that Jesus is coming soon. But after all these years, some begin to wonder.

It is frightening to question whether God can be trusted or not. It sounds a bit blasphemous. But at least asking the question keeps us from being dishonest and from refusing to face tough realities of life.

And one other thing: asking the question puts us in pretty good company, since it is asked often in Scripture.

Laments from the Soul

One of the places where the chirpy tone of "just believe" is questioned is in the book of Lamentations. This rugged book tries to honestly process the worst possible scene in Israel's long history.

King Nebuchadnezzar of Babylon was the dominant power during this period. Actually his powerful empire may not have threatened the existence of Judah if Judah had simply continued paying financial tribute. The prophet Jeremiah pleaded with Zedekiah, king of Judah, to continue payment of taxes to Babylon. Instead Zedekiah, listening to leading officials, took the insane step of renouncing the agreement with Babylon.

Nebuchadnezzar's reaction was swift. Early in 588 B.C., his army arrived, placing Jerusalem under blockade. The "holy city" held out for a year and a half. But then famine struck and Jerusalem was burned and plundered.

The fall of Jerusalem brought an incredible crisis of faith to God's people. Hadn't he promised to protect them? How could he be a faithful God if the Holy of Holies in the temple was being ransacked and the citizens were starving? (A close-up of this faith crisis is found in Psalm 74:1: "Why have you rejected us forever, O God? / Why does your anger smolder against the sheep of your pasture?")

In light of this crisis, the Book of Lamentations is a painful discussion of the question: Can God be trusted? Four of the five chapters of the book are a Hebrew acrostic—perhaps as if to say, "It couldn't get any worse than this. Our agony stretches from A to Z."

Deserted and Desolate

Listen to the cries from the first chapter:

> How deserted lies the city,
>   once so full of people!
> How like a widow is she,
>   who once was great among the nations!
> She who was queen among the provinces
>   has now become a slave (v. 1).
>
> Bitterly she weeps at night,
>   tears are upon her cheeks.
> Among all her lovers
>   there is none to comfort her.
> All her friends have betrayed her;
>   they have become her enemies (v. 2).
>
> The roads to Zion mourn,
>   for no one comes to her appointed feasts.
> All her gateways are desolate,
>   her priests groan,

her maidens grieve,
and she is in bitter anguish (v. 4).

All the splendor has departed
the Daughter of Zion (v. 6a).

The city is allowed to speak of its own destruction later in the chapter as it asks, "Is any suffering like my suffering / that was inflicted on me, / that the Lord brought on me / in the day of his fierce anger?" (v. 12).

Starved and Destroyed

The second chapter describes the fierce anger of the Lord that allowed the fall of Jerusalem: "How the Lord has covered the Daughter of Zion / with the cloud of his anger!" In fact, he is described as the enemy who's been on a rampage.

The writer then surfaces unthinkable tragedies that resulted from the famine. Children and infants had fainted in the streets from lack of nourishment. They asked their mothers where there was food— even "as their lives ebb[ed] away in their mothers' arms" (v. 12). No wonder the writer exclaims, "Your wound is as deep as the sea" (v. 13). The horrors only become worse in the fourth chapter. Not only did children die from starvation, but some parents turned—surely in a state of insanity—to cannibalism:

Those killed by the sword are better off
than those who die of famine;
racked with hunger, they waste away
for lack of food from the field.

With their own hands compassionate women
have cooked their own children,

who became their food
  when my people were destroyed (4: 9, 10).

Beaten and Bitter

The third chapter of Lamentations reads like a personal diary. It tells us how the trauma affected the author. He feels that God has bludgeoned him through the attack on Jerusalem:

He has made my skin and my flesh grow old
  and has broken my bones.
He has besieged me and surrounded me
  with bitterness and hardship.
He has made me dwell in darkness
  like those long dead (v. 4).

Like a bear lying in wait,
  like a lion in hiding,
he dragged me from the path and mangled me
  and left me without help.
He drew his bow
  and made me the target for his arrows.
He pierced my heart
  with arrows from his quiver (vv. 10-13).

He has broken my teeth with gravel;
  he has trampled me in the dust.
I have been deprived of peace;
  I have forgotten what prosperity is.
So I say, "My splendor is gone
  and all that I had hoped from the LORD"
    (vv. 16-18).

Have Your Walls Fallen Down?

As hard as it is to read such words of despair, aren't you glad they're in the Bible? I'm so thankful that when we feel like God has abandoned us, we are a part of a long tradition—all within the community of faith!

While the words from Lamentations may not seem relevant to you right now, wait until *your* walls fall in and the inner sanctuary of *your* life is looted and burned! Ask a teenager whose parents have decided to split. Ask a couple whose business crashed after unbeatable competition moved in just down the street. Ask a victim of a crash who was blindsided by a drunk driver and as a result lost the proper function of her limbs. Ask the family whose reputation has been ruined by vicious lies and misrepresentations.

> *When we feel like God has abandoned us, we are a part of a long tradition—all within the community of faith!*

Is God faithful? Will our prayers be heard? Will the righteous be cared for? Will the Lord keep his promises? Eventually, everyone who lives in reality knows the feeling the author describes in Lamentations—the feeling of being hunted down like a helpless bird. Can you believe when the evidence seems to point against God?

Faith in the Pit

We must read Lamentations long enough to realize that it is not a book of whining. It is a lament. It is an interpretation of a crisis from the vantage point of one in "the depths of the pit" who believes (3:55). The author seeks to make sense of what's happening. From the perspective of faith, he explores the situation, believing there would be no credibility if he didn't deal honestly and painfully with the hurt that had been inflicted.

Lamentations is a magnificent call to realistic faith.

Right in the middle of his weeping, the writer expresses his confident belief that Yahweh is a God of steadfast love. Even the punishment of Israel was an expression of God's love to put the people in a position to receive divine compassion. In the final analysis, Lamentations is a magnificent call to *realistic faith*.

Yet this I call to mind
and therefore I have hope:

Because of the LORD's great love we are not
consumed,
for his compassions never fail.
They are new every morning;
great is your faithfulness.
I say to myself, "The LORD is my portion;
therefore I will wait for him" (3:21-24).

Even though God seems to be silent in answer to the writer's prayers, Jeremiah has learned through God's dealings in history that he is not absent.
Etched on the walls of ruins in Cologne, Germany, is a graffito from World War II. Its words speak of great, biblical faith:

I believe in the sun, even when it's not shining.

I believe in love, even when I don't feel it.
I believe in God, even when he is silent.

Yes, our God who revealed himself most clearly in
Jesus Christ is a faithful God. Friends may leave.
Family members may betray. But our God can
always be trusted. Even when he can't be seen.

Focusing Your Faith

1. What would your reaction have been if you had been living in Jerusalem during the fall of this "holy city"?

2. Describe a time when you experienced soul-wrenching grief, when all your walls came crashing in on you. How did you feel about God during that time?

3. How literally do you think all of God's promises can be taken?

4. When have you felt God failed you by not keeping one of his promises?

5. Recall a time when you could clearly see God's answer to your cry for help. How did his answer affect your view of his trustworthiness?

6. Why is it sometimes hard to see God's answered promises?

7. What do you feel is God's greatest promise?

Chapter 9

False Idea:

God Loves Me

Only

When I'm Good

A few years ago my dad and my best friend spent a morning together jogging. Well, actually only my dad was jogging. My friend was grinning. Even though both are veterans of several marathons, this morning my friend

> **Discovery:**
>
> *God doesn't expect me to be perfect!*

was practicing cardiology, while my father was being put to the test, trying to find out if he needed to worry about some heartbeat irregularities.

So with his best no-one-beats-me-on-this-machine look, my doctor friend kicked on his undefeated treadmill. (Of course, I was there, too. I wouldn't have missed this show for anything!) At first it was a breeze—a nice talkative stroll in central Arkansas. But every couple of minutes the pace changed. The road would get steeper and would move more quickly.

It didn't take long for beads of sweat to start appearing and then running like a tiny creek down my dad's face. And then a few minutes later a dam had burst and the little creek had become the mighty Mississippi. His pulse shot up like a space shuttle. The course became steeper and faster—and less fun. The worst part of this deal is that my dad never got anywhere. He remained in the same spot, just trying not to be thrown off. The treadmill is a wicked machine that has many victories and no defeats!

This is a graphic picture of the lives many Christians lead. In nearly every aspect of their lives, they feel like they're on a treadmill. They can never quite do enough or be quite good enough. And just when they think they are up to speed, someone turns up the machine, and they are playing catch-up again.

Fallout from the Treadmill

We are surrounded by the fallout from the treadmill of "works righteousness." You can see the spiritual exhaustion in some people's faces. They constantly worry about going to hell. "Have I done enough?" "Will I have time for one last prayer before I die?" "Where do I stand on the curve?"

Though they become physically exhausted, they dare not slow down or get off. So instead they seek to pay God off—through church attendance, through good deeds, and through nonstop working. Every sermon they hear on commitment (a needed biblical theme!) only turns up the speed of the machine, makes the course steeper, and makes them think they'll collapse any second. They never feel restful in their relationship with God.

The fallout also strikes the emotional lives of

these weary Christians. Their emotions carry them through a debilitating cycle of guilt, anger, depression, and low self-esteem. Inwardly they can be filled with resentment, rage, self-hate, and self-blame. They refuse to forgive themselves and indulge in self-punishment.

Perhaps the worst part of this whole process is that their lives become filled with garbage. But this garbage doesn't just fill _their_ lives. It seeps out like nuclear waste to contaminate those around. The sufferers package the garbage, put a bow on it, and give it to their children as a present. It eventually brings a putrid smell to marriages, families, and friendships. Since they hate to be on the treadmill alone, they (often unknowingly) try to pull others on with them.

Not only is this treadmill a problem for Christians, it's also a discouragement to those who are watching the performance. Watching my dad on the treadmill certainly didn't make me want to get on it. It was _not_ a pleasant sight. In the same way, many would-be Christians watch us struggle to be perfect. This is not an image that draws people to the Lord. In fact, it causes many to decide not to even try. We make being a Christian look so difficult and tiresome, why would anyone want to attempt it? Just watching us is a workout!

Stuck on the Treadmill

After writing a book about this trap, David Seamands began receiving letters from some of these tired performers:

I have been a struggling Christian for the past thirteen years. My problem is that I am never at

peace and am always trying to be good—that is,
to be better. I am so afraid of making mistakes. . . .

I am a college student and a believer in Christ.
Your article really hit home to me. I am always
feeling that kind of anxiety, guilt, and condemna-
tion. These feelings invade my day-to-day
thought processes. I cannot perform a task, read
a book, or practice my music without feeling I am
being judged. . . . I feel everything I do is not good
enough for my Lord. . . .

It's difficult for me to attend church anymore,
because our minister stresses regular Bible
reading. I want to read God's Word; but whenever
I read the Bible, I feel the Lord is "putting the
whammy on me" for what I am doing and where I
am going with my life. . . . I have all kinds of
unrealistic expectations. Also, I attempt impos-
sible performances and try to get God's approval
by keeping a lot of legalistic rules. I thought I had
to earn his love, and that caused me to almost
take my life. . . .

I want to be used more effectively for the Lord,
but feel so unworthy and useless. I am such a
failure I can't stand to live with myself. . . .

I am a missionary. God has used me to win souls.
I know all the answers, all the Scriptures, and
can quote the exact chapter and verse. But it is
all in my head. The God I serve is never pleased
with me and is certainly nothing like the gracious
loving God I say I believe in—and tell others
about. Why can't I practice what I preach? I feel
like a fake. . . .

I try hard to be loving, but I'm so critical and
judgmental, so hard on my spouse and kids. The

slightest failure on their part and I get angry and explode. Then I feel guilty and get depressed. My family is so loving and forgiving—but that only makes matters worse. It's almost like a pattern that keeps repeating itself. . . .

It seems the harder I try, the harder I fall. When I get exhausted and quit trying at all, I really do feel condemned. . . .[1]

I've included several clips from these letters, because all of us have felt similar sentiments. There are so many of us who affirm grace—who would want to deny it?—but who don't actually live in grace.

Barriers to Accepting Grace

Some have a difficult time accepting the grace of God because of various barriers.

Trying to earn God's approval by our performance is perhaps the oldest and most persistent heresy.

Theological barriers are created when we have digested a steady diet of salvation by human effort— a meal that leaves us bloated but starving.

One woman about my age told me she had recurring dreams of God requiring her to tiptoe across a highwire that has been stretched across a wide, deep canyon. In the dream, Jesus was actually taunting her, trying to make her lose her concentration and fall off. Needless to say, her spiritual life was a disaster—because her God was against her!

Another Christian said that she abhorred the idea

of prayer because for her it was like being called to the principal's office back in junior high. It wasn't likely to be a winning deal.

Trying to earn God's approval by our performance is perhaps the oldest and most persistent heresy. I know so many who refuse the label of legalist but who continue to affirm by their actions that salvation comes from our performance rather than from Jesus' performance.

Trying to earn God's approval by our performance is perhaps the oldest and most persistent heresy.

Even though they know better intellectually, they emotionally imagine God grading on a curve. The grades might be based on obedience or devotional time or evangelistic results or doctrinal accuracy. But however they're measured, these people know they fall short. They live as though God were waiting for them to do a little more, be a little better, precision tune their doctrine. And they're sure he winces as he watches.

Cultural barriers have made it difficult to accept God's incredible message of grace. As Americans we've been schooled in the thinking of self-reliance; you get what you need by your own individual effort. You earn your pay, earn respect, and earn a promotion. In other cultures, an aged person would proudly announce at the center of the village that her children are caring for her in her old age. But in our society, many are ashamed to admit that their middle-aged children are having to help them out in their retirement years.

The atmosphere of self-reliance is also regularly swept by the winds of activism: "God helps those who help themselves." This philosophy doesn't mix well with the gospel story, where God helps those who can't help themselves (Romans 5:6-8).

Experiential barriers cause many to choke on the pure, sparkling water of grace. We are all born with basic emotional needs that should be met in families—needs like unconditional love, acceptance, and security. If these needs aren't met, we can be doubtful that anyone—even God—would offer us such love and acceptance.

And, of course, because those needs haven't been filled, many people are hungry for something that they aren't sure exists. For some it's because of physical or emotional abuse at home. For others it's because their parents were too busy to make them feel secure. Many times I've heard college students say, "My folks gave me everything I needed—everything but love."

Many people are hungry for
something that they aren't sure exists.

For others grace comes hard because they were raised in a home that held up unattainable standards. Their parents could never be pleased. In some of these homes, affection was withheld as a means of punishment, or guilt was used as a means of control. (One thirty-something woman said she had been on a long guilt trip with her mom as the travel agent.) In these families, the message that says "your behavior was not acceptable" was often translated "*you* are not acceptable."

David Seamands tells of a woman named Margaret who as an adult displayed outbursts of anger and depression that were ruining her marriage. When he began helping her, he found that she was being controlled by an internal voice from the past—the voice of her perfectionist mother who was never quite satisfied. And somehow this voice had become the displeased voice of God.

She recalled her first piano recital, and how she wanted to play perfectly so her mom would be happy. So she practiced until her fingers nearly fell off. When the recital came, she performed flawlessly. As she got up from the bench, her piano instructor grabbed her elbow and said, "Excellent, Margaret; you played it perfectly!" But when she took her place next to her mother, her mom leaned over and whispered, "Your slip was showing the whole time." Now to her God was the Eternal Parent who kept whispering that her slip was showing.[2]

Get off the Treadmill

Many people never realize or accept that they can get off of the treadmill. What can be done to help such people? Unfortunately, our culture is so thoroughly penetrated by the therapeutic model that many think they're forever tied to the past. Armed with a new vocabulary of words such as dysfunction, dependency, codependency, addiction, and denial (all very helpful within a proper Christian framework), they become victims of the past.

The good news that Christianity offers is that we can get off the treadmill. Through spiritual healing, through Christian guidance or counseling, and through a renewed understanding of God, we can be delivered from such deadly treadmill theology.

In Titus 3:3, Paul explains why we'll never be able to play the treadmill game well enough: "At one time we too were foolish, disobedient, deceived and enslaved by all kinds of passions and pleasures. We lived in malice and envy, being hated and hating one another." Because of sin, we can't earn our salvation. Not just specific sins, but SIN—the destructive, pervading power of evil that has captured every person.

The good news that Christianity offers is that we can get off the treadmill.

Paul, a veteran of "treadmillism," understood all too well how far from God one can be while appearing to be very spiritual. Everyone, he tells us, has chosen to participate in the fallenness of our world, regardless of credentials or prior performance. But then he explains how this gap can be filled. Not by jumping as far as we can. Not by tiptoeing across a highwire. The gap is filled by a bridge that God, out of his stupendous grace, constructed through the sacrifice of his Son—a bridge in the shape of a cross.

But when the kindness and love of God our Savior appeared, he saved us, not because of righteous things we had done, but because of his mercy. He saved us through the washing of rebirth and renewal by the Holy Spirit, whom he poured out on us generously through Jesus Christ our Savior, so that, having been justified by his grace, we might become heirs having the hope of eternal life (Titus 3:4-7).

The grace of God fills the pages of both testaments.

It is the glue that holds the biblical story together. And that grace has been shown most clearly and powerfully through the death and resurrection of Jesus Christ. We are saved not because of our ability to stay on the treadmill but because of what God has done through Jesus. The status of his followers now is that of heirs.

What incredible news! If I die this week, I'll spend eternity with God in heaven.

What incredible news! If I die this week, I'll spend eternity with God in heaven. I might be wrong concerning some details about worship or some minor doctrinal issue. But I will still be with God. I might fall short of where I should be in reaching lost people for the Lord. But I'm still saved.

This doesn't deny that there's a response to grace. "For the grace of God has appeared, bringing salvation to all" (Titus 2:11, NRSV). We must respond with obedience, service, sacrifice, and good works, not to win God's approval or to repay him, but to express our thanks to God for his grace and to trust him with the guidance of our lives. We grow in these matters because he loves us, accepts us, forgives us.

Collapse into Kind Arms

In 1793 William Carey, "the father of modern missions," left behind his life in England to go to India. There he invested his life in translating Scripture, organizing evangelistic teams, and teaching others. But at his request his gravestone reads simply:

WILLIAM CAREY
Born August 17th, 1761
Died June, 1834
A wretched, poor and helpless worm,
On Thy kind arms I fall.

If you are one of the exhausted Christians I've described in this chapter, if you're weary of trying to earn your salvation, if you're tired of worrying about being lost, then go ahead and get off the treadmill. And don't worry about falling. The kind arms of God are there to catch you!

Notes:

1. David A. Seamands, _Freedom from the Performance Trap_ (Wheaton: Victor Books, 1988). Used by permission.
2. Ibid.

Focusing Your Faith

1. Describe your "treadmill" experience.

2. What is dangerous about getting off the tread-mill? How does God's grace make it easier to get off?

3. God still expects us to live a "good life," doesn't he? How can we balance this with grace?

4. In what ways do we cheapen God's grace?

5. If "the treadmill" is a problem for you, what kind of "exercise training program" should you be on?

6. What kinds of things is your Eternal Parent whispering in your ear?

7. When you go on a guilt trip, who is usually your travel agent? How can you change that?

Chapter 10

False Idea:

Even God Can't
Fix My Mess

A friend of mine, visiting a church in another state, was surprised to hear that there would be a "business meeting" following the assembly to discuss a problem. The relative whom he had gone with asked him to stay,

Discovery:

God's power is unlimited.

promising it shouldn't take too long.

But the discussion didn't take long to change from a slight disagreement to nuclear war. Anger filled the air like heavy smog as hurt feelings from many years spewed out. Just when it looked like Armageddon had arrived, an older gentleman suggested that those present pause to pray for God's help and wisdom. Immediately the minister retorted, "Has it come to that?"

I doubt that any Christian would intellectually

deny the strength of God. Everyone knows that God
is omnipotent. We know it, yet we just don't believe
it! It's in our reliance upon God's power—or our lack
of reliance—that we discover whether we truly
believe in him or not.

Is the Lord's Arm Too Short?

In Numbers 11, the people of Israel begin whining about how good life had been back in Egypt.
(Isn't it amazing how short our memories can be?)
They had eaten all the manna casserole they could
stand. They were craving the fish, cucumbers, mel-
ons, and spices from Egypt.

When Moses pleads with the LORD, he is told that
the people will have meat for a whole month. Moses
finds that hard to believe, given their large number
and meager resources:

> Here I am among six hundred thousand men on
> foot, and you say, "I will give them meat to eat for
> a whole month!" Would they have enough if flocks
> and herds were slaughtered for them? Would
> they have enough if all the fish in the sea were
> caught for them (vv. 21, 22)?

Didn't Moses know that God is a mighty God? Of
course. He'd witnessed God's power in the sending of
the plagues and the crossing of the sea. The struggle
came in believing that God could and would help
him in this particular situation.

The Lord's response was penetrating: "Is the
LORD's arm too short?" (v. 23) In other words, "Don't
you believe I can pull it off, Moses?" That's the
question we face: Can he take care of me no matter
what *my* situation may be?

❖ This question is asked by those trying to
rebuild after a devastating loss—death,
divorce, tragedy—efforts akin to trying to
scale up Colorado's Pike's Peak.

❖ It's asked by those who've been trapped by
a sin and who are now trying to turn their
lives around—which is similar to turning
an ocean liner with an oar.

❖ It's asked by those who, in trying to put a
marriage back together after months and
years of conflict, feel like they're trying to
put together a jigsaw puzzle with a million
pieces—while wearing mittens.

❖ It's asked by some who are trying to forgive people who have hurt them deeply
when they don't feel very forgiving and
when there are no signs of repentance and
sorrow on the part of those they're trying
to forgive.

Not only do we face the challenge of believing
God's power can help us in our personal and family
lives, we find it difficult to credit God's power to
work in our church families. How, for example, can
we think about church renewal when the forces of
tradition are more powerful than gravity—unless we
rely on the power of God? How can we dare dream of
evangelizing the world when the powers of evil seem
so great—unless we put our hope in the God whose
arm isn't too short?

Power of Inner Strength

A few years ago when Stacy King was a rookie
basketball player with the Chicago Bulls, he got in

the game the evening Michael Jordan scored 69 points. After the game, when asked for his reflections on the night, he said, "I'll always remember it as the evening Michael Jordan and I combined for 70 points." His humorous response pointed out that even though he was in the game, the real fire power came from the superstar.

He provides the power as we provide the willingness.

Similarly, people who trust in the God of Scripture believe that they are indwelt by one who has more power than they can imagine. Paul encourages the church in Ephesus with these words:

> I pray that out of his glorious riches he may strengthen you with power through his Spirit in your inner being, so that Christ may dwell in your hearts through faith. And I pray that you, being rooted and established in love, may have power, together with all the saints, to grasp how wide and long and high and deep is the love of Christ, and to know this love that surpasses knowledge—that you may be filled to the measure of all the fullness of God (Ephesians 3:16-19).

We can forgive when we don't have the power to forgive; we can survive in life when we feel like we're sinking; we can overcome sin when we don't have the strength to overcome. The God who created the heavens and earth is working through us. He provides the power as we provide the willingness. That's why Paul prayed that believers might know God's "incomparably great power for us who believe. That power is like the working of his mighty strength, which he exerted in Christ when he raised him from the dead and seated him at his right hand in the heavenly realms" (Ephesians 1:19, 20).

Can God Bring His People Home?

In the Book of Isaiah, the wind changes directions in chapter 40. There is an announcement that the Israelites, who are in exile in Babylon, will get to go home. The section ends in Isaiah 55:1 with the invitation:

> Come, all you who are thirsty,
>   come to the waters;
> and you who have no money,
>   come, buy and eat!

But when this unbelievable invitation was sent out, can you imagine the people's response? "Can God really pull it off?" Again, it wasn't so much an intellectual query as a faith struggle.

There's No Comparison!

The text answers: "See, the Sovereign LORD comes with power, / and his arm rules for him" (40:10).

The LORD's strength is spotlighted by comparisons that run through the rest of the chapter. "To whom, then, will you compare God?" (v. 18).

The Nations Are Nothing?

God's enormous power is highlighted first by comparing him to the mightiest nations of the world:

> Surely the nations are like a drop in a bucket;
>   they are regarded as dust on the scales;

he weighs the islands as though they were fine
dust.
Lebanon is not sufficient for altar fires,
nor its animals enough for burnt offerings.
Before him all the nations are as nothing;
they are regarded by him as worthless
and less than nothing (Isaiah 40:15-17).

Israel, Egypt, Babylon, Persia, Greece, Rome,
Germany, Russia, the U.S.A., China, Japan—all
have been or are mighty nations. But they are just
drops in the bucket, just dust on the scales, when
compared with God.

After church services, some of the children will
recycle our church bulletins by making paper air-
planes. If you took one of them out to the air force
base and placed it next to an F-16 fighter plane, that
would be similar to putting the most powerful nation
of the world next to God. It fails miserably in the
comparison.

How Do Idols Stack Up?

The contrast continues as the true God is compared with pathetic idols:

To whom, then, will you compare God?
What image will you compare him to?
As for an idol, a craftsman casts it,
and a goldsmith overlays it with gold
and fashions silver chains for it.
A man too poor to present such an offering
selects wood that will not rot.
He looks for a skilled craftsman
to set up an idol that will not topple.
Isaiah 40:18-20

A humorous description of the making of an idol

continues in chapter 44:

> [A man] cut down cedars,
>   or perhaps took a cypress or oak.
> He let it grow among the trees of the forest,
>   or planted a pine, and the rain made it grow.
> It is man's fuel for burning;
>   some of it he takes and warms himself,
>   he kindles a fire and bakes bread.
> But he also fashions a god and worships it;
>   he makes an idol and bows down to it.
> Half of the wood he burns in the fire;
>   over it he prepares his meal,
>   he roasts his meat and eats his fill.
> He also warms himself and says,
>   "Ah! I am warm; I see the fire."
> From the rest he makes a god, his idol;
>   he bows down to it and worships.
> He prays to it and says,
>   "Save me; you are my god" (vv. 14-17).

The prophet can't believe it! No one stopped to think about how ridiculous it was to use half of the wood for fuel and then to bow down before the other half.

***God's power over other gods is shown
throughout the Old Testament.***

God's power over other gods is shown throughout the Old Testament. In Exodus 1-12, the contest is not so much between Moses and Pharaoh as between God and the gods of Egypt. Those gods should have been able to defend their turf, but they couldn't. They were no match for the Lord Almighty.

Dagon, a god of the Philistines, appeared mighty and awesome until the ark of the covenant was carried into his temple. But overnight the statue of Dagon fell on his face. When the Philistines found him they put him back in his place. But the next morning they found him down on his face again (in a position of submissiveness!) with his head and hands broken off. He literally couldn't stand up to the power of Yahweh.

Perhaps the clearest contest in the Old Testament is told in 1 Kings 18. There Elijah stood against 450 prophets of Baal and four hundred prophets of Asherah in a test to see whose God was greater. Which one, Yahweh or Baal, would be able to bring fire to the altar?

The LORD—he is God!

When the prophets of Baal prayed and danced themselves into a frenzy, all to no avail, Elijah revealed what a good sense of humor he had. "Shout louder!" he said. "Surely [Baal] is a god! Perhaps he is deep in thought, or busy, or traveling. Maybe he is sleeping and must be awakened" (18:27). So the devotees went into a greater frenzy, even slashing themselves until they were bleeding—but "there was no response, no one answered, no one paid attention" (v. 29).

Then Elijah had water from the Mediterranean brought to the top of Mount Carmel and poured over the altar. "The water ran down around the altar and even filled the trench" (v. 35). The text gives a graphic description of what happened next: "Then the fire of the LORD fell and burned up the sacrifice, the wood, the stones and the soil, and also licked up the water in the trench" (v. 38). The people fell down before him and cried, "The LORD—he is God! The Lord—he is God!" (v. 39).

Can World Rulers Compete?

A third comparison in Isaiah 40 is to the mighty rulers of the world. When we think of powerful individuals, we may picture some of the muscled hulks on television. Have you ever seen the monsters on "American Gladiators," for example? Their arms are as big as my thighs, their legs as big as my waist, and their bodies are covered with hair. And those are the women. You should see the men! Others may think of CEOs of large corporations, billionaires, or sports figures.

But to Isaiah's audience, the best portrait of power was the earthly rulers of the day. And, yet, even they don't begin to compare with God:

> He brings princes to naught
>> and reduces the rulers of this world to
>>> nothing.
> No sooner are they planted,
>> no sooner are they sown,
>> no sooner do they take root in the ground,
> than he blows on them and they wither,
>> and a whirlwind sweeps them away like
>>> chaff (vv. 23, 24).

These are people who wield great power on earth. But they topple like Humpty-Dumpty: Solomon, Nebuchadnezzar, Caesar, Alexander, Charlemagne, Napoleon, Hitler, Lincoln, Roosevelt—you name it. Eventually you have to find them in an encyclopedia or history book. But God's name and his power are as current today as ever.

Is Your God Too Middle-Sized?

How fitting that the Holy One of Israel then asks, "To whom will you compare me? / Or who is my equal?" (v. 25). In C. S. Lewis's *Prince Caspian*, one of the books in the classic Chronicles of Narnia series, Lucy comments on how much larger Aslan—the lion who represents Christ—is than when she last saw him. And Aslan replies, "I am not. But every year you grow you will find me bigger."

That's exactly how it is with God. When we're young, we're told that God has all power. But as we grow, we should see more and more evidence of how true that is.

When our vision of God diminishes or fails to grow, Christianity becomes a tame, drab, lukewarm, safe religion that fits comfortably into our malnourished worldview.

Unfortunately, many people have their vision of God's power cloud as they get older. Some feel defeated. Others feel knocked down by the force of sin. And still others develop a human-centered, highly rational faith that keeps God at a distance. Over thirty years ago, J. B. Phillips wrote a little book entitled *Your God Is Too Small*. Perhaps it needs to be brought up to date with a companion volume: *Your God Is Too Middle-Sized*.

When our vision of God diminishes or fails to grow, Christianity becomes a tame, drab, lukewarm, safe religion that fits comfortably into our malnourished worldview.

Look Again

Let us open our eyes again to catch a glimpse of the power of God that is working in the lives of his people:

Do you not know?
  Have you not heard?
The LORD is the everlasting God,
  the Creator of the ends of the earth.
He will not grow tired or weary,
  and his understanding no one can fathom.
He gives strength to the weary
  and increases the power of the weak.
Even youths grow tired and weary,
  and young men stumble and fall;
but those who hope in the LORD
  will renew their strength.
They will soar on wings like eagles;
  they will run and not grow weary,
  they will walk and not be faint.
                    Isaiah 40:28-31

Are you one who always feels dirty because you can't imagine God removing _your_ sin? Then look again at his power!

Are you one who has been fighting a losing battle with some addictive sin—drugs, alcohol, immorality, envy, pride, anger? Then look again to his strength!

Are you one who is weary of trying to put your life back together after being abused, attacked, or abandoned? Then fix your eyes on the One who called the world into existence and who lives in you through his Spirit!

Our God is not an abstract God, a distant God, a silent God, a feeble God. He is the Almighty Ruler who spoke all things into existence, the Victorious Warrior who conquered the forces of evil through his Son at the cross, the Lord of All who indwells his people through his Spirit.

Now to him who is able to do immeasurably more than all we ask or imagine, according to his power that is at work within us, to him be glory in the church and in Christ Jesus throughout all generations, for ever and ever! Amen (Ephesians 3:20, 21).

Focusing Your Faith

1. Why do people tend to make God small?

2. Why does it seem that Christ grows stronger as we grow spiritually?

3. Which problems are difficult for you to hand over to God?

4. What specific problem do you especially have difficulty giving over to God?

5. How does it make you feel to know that God's power is available to you and that you can call on it at any time?

6. After pleading with the Lord for weeks about something, how surprised were you when he actually gave you what you asked for? Did you tell anyone what God did for you?

7. This week, keep a prayer journal. Write down everything you prayed for each day. One week later look over your journal and record how he answered each request.

PART 3:

DARE TO DISCOVER THE GOD YOU'VE NEVER KNOWN

Chapter 11

Discover:

The
Approachable King

Many specific roles
and attributes of God
have been discussed
throughout this book.
One common biblical
description of God which
encompasses all of these,
and perhaps even more,
is that of God as king.

> **Discovery:**
>
> *I can come to God
> with anything.*

We may not easily
see a connection for our lives today; we may not
recognize our hunger for a king. However, people in
biblical times understood at both a rational and an
emotional level what it meant to be a king, to need a
king, and to serve a king. They were familiar with
King David or King Hezekiah or King Cyrus or King
Herod.

The first thing the Israelites did after arriving in
their new homeland was to start asking for a king.
They claimed that everyone else had one and that

they needed a king to be their symbol of power and unity. This king could lead them into battle and protect these vulnerable Israelites from their enemies. In return, the Israelites would owe the king their loyalty, their service, and much of their money.

Reverence for Royalty

But Americans have never lived in a monarchy. We have a hard time even imagining the dignity and reverence reserved for royalty. Perhaps in pre-Watergate days, we experienced a hint of such reverence. In those days, the press protected the gravity of FDR's illness because "he was the president." Likewise, many in the press hushed the reports of Kennedy's extramarital affairs because he was the chief executive of our country. Whether you liked the leader or not, he was still our president and deserved our utmost respect.

In post-Watergate days such patriotic respect is long gone. Comedians imitate presidents' peculiar habits and expressions and delight in poking fun at the presidents' wives. The press exposes their mistakes and inadequacies, and TV crews record and rerun their every mishap. You probably remember the networks' feverish detailing of George Bush's throwing up at a state dinner in Japan. American presidents are certainly not treated with reverence.

What, then, would it be like to be in the presence of royalty? Don Jackson, one of the elders at our church, served part of his career in government as senior U.S. liaison officer to the Court of Saint James. Here is his personal description of being called into the presence of the queen of England:

I was aware of a commotion outside of my office

window at the American Embassy in London. I
looked out the window and saw a royal carriage
painted in red and gold and drawn by four magnificent, matched, dapple-gray horses, and accompanied by a troop of Royal Grenadiers.

I returned to my desk, and shortly my secretary
appeared at the door and said, "You have a
guest." She stepped back to reveal a gentleman
dressed in red and gold, highly bemedaled,
bewigged, and carrying a mace which he pounded
on the floor three times. Then he unfurled a scroll
and began to read:

> Elizabeth II, by the Grace of God, of the
> United Kingdom of Great Britain and North-
> ern Ireland and of Her Other Realms and
> Territories, Queen, Head of the Common-
> wealth, Defender of the Faith
>
> Commands
> The Lord Chamberlain
> To Invite
> Dr. and Mrs. Don Jackson
> To an Evening Reception at
> Buckingham Palace
> on Wednesday, 26th November 1980,
> at 7:30 p.m.
> Evening Dress with Decorations

Again, he pounded the floor three times and
stepped back. Then another gentleman, also in
royal uniform, appeared in the doorway and
identified himself as the Royal Marshall of the
Diplomatic Corps—and may he please have some
of my time, he asked. We sat down, and he instructed me for over an hour on how to be pre-
sented to Her Majesty, the queen. This guidance

included my dress, which had to be British white tie and tails. He also instructed me on how my wife was to dress—in a full-length gown with a high neck and white gloves above the elbow. For about fifteen or twenty minutes he instructed me on subjects appropriate to discuss with the queen and her royal family. He went on with instructions about how to address each member of the family. When he left, he gave me a book with guidelines on how to meet Her Majesty and how to behave in her presence. Later when I asked why we were told exactly how to dress and what subjects we might speak about, I was answered, "Because that's what the queen wants." End of discussion.

Finally the night of the royal dinner and the royal reception came. We appeared at the grand entry of Buckingham Palace and were met by a troop of the Life Guards, each over six-foot-two. Each one was bewigged and was carrying a spear, and they escorted us into the palace which was designed by John Nash in the 1700s.

After a tour of the palace, we arrived at the Throne Room and awaited the queen's arrival. Shortly she did arrive, dressed in a magnificent gown and adorned with royal jewelry. As she entered the room, everyone stood out of respect. Then came the introductions to the queen when we could pay our respects. And I tell you that it was most impressive for this old country boy from Oklahoma to see what majesty meant.

Now that gives us a vivid image of royalty. But as Americans it's still difficult to understand. Not long ago Queen Elizabeth II visited Washington, D.C., during her tour of the city, she visited a shelter for abused women. One of the ladies there, overcome with emotion and excitement, lunged toward the queen in an effort to hug her. The queen did not respond favorably, however, and her aides quickly removed the woman. The British were horrified that Americans would be so uninformed on regal manners, while Americans were insulted at the queen's coldness.

Hero Worship

Actually, people in America today do hunger for a king, for a hero, to identify with and imitate. From sports heroes to rock stars, companies knock themselves out trying to get these people to use and promote their products. They know that these people possess a powerful influence over the masses.

People in America today do hunger for a king, for a hero, to identify with and imitate.

We want to be identified with a successful winner, so we wear certain types of clothes, drive certain types of cars, go on certain types of diets, and even give to certain types of charities. Through the ages people have always chosen a king to worship, whether it's a person of royal blood, an athlete, money, or fame. And whom they worship as king states who and whose they are.

Those of us who serve and worship the living God are called to be in the presence of a much higher authority than the queen of England or a much greater hero than any sports figure. He is the Winner of winners; he is the King of kings and Lord of lords. Yet God doesn't have lists of rules and regulations to meet before we can approach him. Instead, this King requires love and honor for commoners as well as for himself. We can come to him anytime to satisfy our hunger for a king in our life. We can rejoice and join with the psalmists to celebrate his kingship:

> Clap your hands, all you nations;
> shout to God with cries of joy.
> How awesome is the LORD Most High,
> the great King over all the earth! . . .
> For God is the King of all the earth;
> sing to him a psalm of praise.
> Psalm 47: 1, 2, 7

> Great and marvelous are your deeds,
> Lord God Almighty.
> Just and true are your ways,
> King of the ages.
> Who will not fear you, O Lord,
> and bring glory to your name?
> For you alone are holy.
> All nations will come
> and worship before you,
> for your righteous acts have been revealed.
> Revelation 15:3, 4

As Scripture points us to this king, what are we learning about him, and how are we coming to know him better?

His Cosmic Kingdom

First, the supreme kingship of God implies that

he and he alone rules the universe. He has no rival.
He is the sovereign majesty who deserves all glory
and praise.

Several of the psalms are known as enthronement psalms. They announce the worthiness of God
to be king. They proclaim that he is over all the
nations, not just Israel:

> For God is the King of all the earth . . .
> God reigns over the nations;
>   God is seated on his holy throne.
> The nobles of the nations assemble
>   as the people of the God of Abraham,
> for the kings of the earth belong to God;
>   he is greatly exalted.
>   Psalm 47:7-9

The God of Scripture is not a private or even a
national God. He isn't a genie in a bottle whom we
can magically call for our own purposes, nor is he a
jack-in-the-box whom we can shove back in when
we're through with him. He rules all the countries,
all the peoples of the world.

He also rules over all the "gods" of the nations.
They pale in comparison to him.

> For the LORD is the great God,
>   the great King above all gods.
>   Psalm 95:3

Whether these gods are called Marduk, Molech,
and Baal, or Money, Sex, and Power, they cannot
compete with God Almighty.

The psalms also announce God's rule over all
nature:

> The seas have lifted up, O LORD,

the seas have lifted up their voice;
the seas have lifted up their pounding waves.
Mightier than the thunder of the great waters,
mightier than the breakers of the sea—
the LORD on high is mighty.
Psalm 93:3, 4

Let the heavens rejoice, let the earth be glad;
let the sea resound, and all that is in it;
let the fields be jubilant, and everything in
them.
Then all the trees of the forest will sing for joy.
Psalm 96:11, 12

Let the sea resound, and everything in it,
the world, and all who live in it.
Let the rivers clap their hands,
let the mountains sing together for joy;
let them sing before the LORD . . . .
Psalm 98:7-9a

The description is cosmic, global, expansive.
Sometimes we say we are going to begin worship.
But if we understand the language of these psalms,
we can't begin worship; we can only participate in
the worship that already exists. There is praise of
God that comes from the mountains, the rivers, the
fields—even the rocks can cry out!

God is sovereign over all creation. He wants
everyone and everything to submit willfully and
joyfully to his rule. But whether they do or not, he is
still their ruler. No wonder, then, that when Isaiah
saw "the Lord seated on a throne, high and exalted"
(Isaiah 6:1) he could only cry out: "I am ruined! For I
am a man of unclean lips, and I live among a people
of unclean lips, and my eyes have seen the King, the

Lord Almighty" (v. 5). In the presence of such all-consuming majesty, no other response is possible.

Nebuchadnezzar's Dream

The fourth chapter of Daniel provides a graphic example of one who sought to ignore the kingship of God. Nebuchadnezzar, the powerful ruler of Babylon, envisioned a stunning tree growing in the middle of the land. It was a living skyscraper that provided both fruit and shelter. But as the dream continued, he saw "a holy one coming down from heaven" who demanded that the tree be cut down, pruned of its branches and stripped of its leaves. Only a stump was to remain.

---

*There is no such thing as a
self-made man.*

Daniel's heart jumped into his throat because he knew the dream was an indictment of the dreamer who sought his interpretation. But he boldly told Nebuchadnezzar that he was the tree who would be leveled if he didn't acknowledge "that the Most High is sovereign over the kingdoms of men and gives them to anyone he wishes" (v. 17). His advice was pointed: "Renounce your sins by doing what is right, and your wickedness by being kind to the oppressed" (v. 27).

Eventually we must all be confronted with the sinfulness of our destructive desire to rule our own lives and take credit where credit isn't due. There is no such thing as a self-made man. We must all learn, although maybe not so suddenly and dramatically as Nebuchadnezzer, that the king of the universe cannot be rivaled.

You'd think Nebuchadnezzar would repent. But like most of us, a night or two of sleep can let the best intentions slip away. So roll the calendar forward twelve months and picture him strolling out on the roof of his royal palace. Hear his proud remark: "Is not this the great Babylon I have built as the royal residence, by my mighty power and for the glory of my majesty?" (v. 30). What arrogance— arrogance that brought the dream to reality.

Immediately the king of Babylon was driven away from his subjects into a field where he ate grass like a cow. Then "his body was drenched with the dew of heaven until his hair grew like the feathers of an eagle and his nails like the claws of a bird" (v. 33). How the mighty have fallen!

Anyone who grasps the significance
of God as king has no choice but to
repent and worship.

But at last Nebuchadnezzar finally came to his senses. He recaptured his sanity. "Then," he said, "I praised the Most High; I honored and glorified him who lives forever. . . . Now I, Nebuchadnezzar, praise and exalt and glorify the King of heaven, because everything he does is right and all his ways are just. And those who walk in pride he is able to humble" (vv. 34, 37). Anyone who grasps the significance of God as king has no choice but to repent and worship.

Rest in His Grasp

The description of God as royal ruler also helps us understand that he protects his people. When

Scripture says that he is enthroned between the cherubim (Psalm 99:1), it means that he is seated on the ark of the covenant. This ark is his throne and the chariot on which he rides as he leads his people into battle (Numbers 10:35; Joshua 6, 7; 1 Samuel 4). He would not abandon his people; rather, he would be the one fighting for them, their true source of strength.

He also protects his people by preserving justice:

Can a corrupt throne be allied with you—
    one that brings on misery by its decrees?
They band together against the righteous
    and condemn the innocent to death.
But the LORD has become my fortress,
    and my God the rock in whom I take refuge.
He will repay them for their sins
    and destroy them for their wickedness;
    the LORD our God will destroy them.
                        Psalm 94:20-23

The King is mighty, he loves justice—
    you have established equity;
in Jacob you have done
    what is just and right.
Exalt the LORD our God
    and worship at his footstool;
    he is holy.
                        Psalm 99:4, 5

Because God is a just king, we can entrust our lives to him. We can let our lives rest in his powerful grasp.

Recently a bungee jumping business came to our flat West Texas city. Since there are no cliffs to dive off, any adventuresome soul who has fifty dollars and no sense is lifted up to a 100-foot platform. Then he jumps—for the fun of it.

Having a touch of acrophobia, I'm more likely to hand-feed a rat to a rattlesnake than I am to bungee jump. But I admire their trust—diving off the cliff or platform, believing that the cord around their ankle or waist is going to keep them from drilling a new hole in the earth's crust.

Still, if I take a free-falling plunge, I want it to be the plunge of faith. Since God is the King of the universe, he is more than able to keep me secure. My life is safe in his hands. As old-time evangelist Marshall Keeble put it: "If God tells me to jump through a brick wall, it's up to me to jump. It's up to God to make the hole!"

Jesus Delivers the Kingdom

To proclaim that God is King also signifies that he is moving history toward his grand conclusion. While Babylonian hymns "enthrone" their gods for the seasonal cycles, the enthronement psalms of Scripture point to God's purposeful work in history.

---

*The victory continues—because
he is KING!*

The New Testament underscores this view of history. It claims that while God has always been king, he intervened in a unique way by the sending of Jesus.

Danish philosopher Soren Kierkegaard told a story of a king who became a peasant for a year. When the people discovered his attempt at commonality, they adored him.

This is the story of Jesus, the royal one who
"emptied himself" to become a servant among men
and women. Could the people in Jerusalem, watching Jesus ride into town on a donkey, have had any
idea how true was their pronouncement, "Blessed is
the king who comes in the name of the Lord!" (Luke
19:38)?

The death and resurrection of Jesus set in motion
an unchangeable chain of events that will ultimately
climax in the deliverance of the kingdom back to God
when the final enemy, death, has its last breath
squeezed out (1 Corinthians 15:28). We now live in
the "in between" time—after the victory was accom-
plished but before the final mopping up has been
completed. And what a triumphant time to live!
Because like Mary and the disciples, we live on
through his death and resurrection. The victory
continues—because he is KING!

Rely on His Rescue

What response could possibly be made to the
King of kings and Lord of lords except full devotion?
Knowing God as king means trusting him, relying on
him, and giving ourselves day by day to his reign.

When the people of Israel came to Gideon asking
that he become their king to protect them, Gideon's
response was that neither he nor his son would
become their king (Judges 8). He reminded them
that they already had a king—the One who had
brought them out of Egypt. They didn't need to
anoint a king; rather, they needed to acknowledge
the King who already ruled.

Scripture urges us to turn our lives over to this
Majestic One. It pleads with us to realize that we
can't rule our lives well until we realize that we can't

rule our lives at all. Only God, in his sovereign tenderness, can satisfy our hunger for protection. Only God can be entrusted to rescue us.

Focusing Your Faith

1. Do you talk to God formally or intimately? How would it change the way you talk to God if he had dictated lengthy, formal instructions on how to approach him?

2. In what ways is God not like a king?

3. Who were your heroes as a child? Why did you look up to them?

4. In what ways do you find yourself patterning your life after worldly heroes today?

5. We all feel helpless and vulnerable sometimes and need our King to save us. In what way has God rescued you recently?

6. Other than God, who (or what) has been the king of your life?

7. Read again Psalm 47; then sing a song of praise to your King.

Chapter 12

Discover:

The God Who
Changes the Unchangeable

Philip Yancey has described it as one of the ugliest words in our language. It is a word that nearly suffocates all the joy out of life.

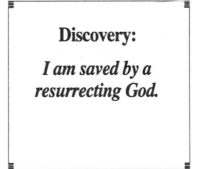

Discovery:

I am saved by a resurrecting God.

The word is *irreversible*. Like when you were ten and foolishly agreed to get on the monster roller coaster, then begged, a bit too late, to get off. Or like when you walk into the Cliffhanger at Six Flags that takes you up slowly for what seems like a couple of miles, pauses (long enough for you to wonder, Do I have disability insurance?), and then drops you.

Perhaps you missed the shot with two seconds to play in the district tournament. Or you turned down a job that you wish you'd taken but now is filled by someone else.

Victims of Irreversibility

We all would like to do a few things over,
wouldn't we? Wouldn't it be nice if life provided a
delete button like the one on the computer—a button
that would allow you to start afresh? Or wouldn't
you like it if real life provided Mulligans—when
golfers get a second chance to better their shot?

Wouldn't you love to re-do some things that are
now irreversible? Haven't you written some things in
ink which you wish you'd have written in lead so you
could erase? Aren't there a few words you've spoken
in anger that you wish you could retract? Haven't
you sent a letter or two you later wished you could
have pulled out of the mailbox? Haven't you experienced a relationship or two where the sweet taste of
companionship suddenly turned sour?

Irreversible—it really is an ugly word. I remember feeling its painfulness when I was twelve and
was told early on a Sunday morning that my grandfather had died suddenly. I wished I could be like
Superman, a hero who could reverse time by flying
backward fast enough to change the earth's rotation.
But I couldn't do that. I couldn't go back and protect
my grandfather.

I saw its ugliness when I told a young woman
that her husband, my good friend, had suddenly
died, leaving her a widow and their infant fatherless. Another friend went with me to the funeral
home and became physically sick upon viewing the
body. It was so obscenely final. So irreversible.

I've scented the stench of irreversibility in the
slow death of a dear friend over the past year who
suffered with AIDS. I've seen its ugliness in the
shared pain of families at Boys' Town and other
children's clinics: families trying to find out what is

wrong with their children.

Some have suffered the loss of dreams that turned upside down into nightmares: marriages made in heaven that unraveled in purgatory; victims of violent, intrusive crimes who keep wishing they could remove the horror.

Most of us could stand pain if it didn't seem to be so relentless, so inescapable!

Jesus Understands

When God became flesh he experienced, eyeball-to-eyeball, the agony of life's irreversibility. He was torn apart inside by the grief of a widow whose only son had died (Luke 7). He heard the tortured cry of a woman whose brother had died: "If you had been here, my brother would not have died" (John 11:21).

When God became flesh he experienced, eyeball-to-eyeball, the agony of life's irreversibility.

Nothing is more irreversible than the grave. Nothing is more hopeless and drab. The crypt tells no tales.

We hear the day Jesus died called "Good Friday." But it became "good" only in the rearview mirror of Christian history. At the time it was the end of dreams. He was nailed to a cross, taken down, and placed in a cold, damp tomb.

When Mary, the mother of Jesus, cried at the foot of the cross, with pain so deep for her son, she surely felt the greatest measure of hopelessness a woman can feel. Along with his cruel, unjust death, died her hopes and dreams.

Christ Is Risen!

Philip Yancey tells the story of Rollo May, the famous therapist, who suffered a complete nervous breakdown when in his twenties. His road to recovery, documented in his book, *The Quest for Beauty*, involved continual encounters with beauty.

The encounters included a visit to a monastery on Mount Athos, a peninsula attached to Greece. One morning May happened onto the celebration of the Greek Orthodox Easter. The only light in the sanctuary came from candles. The air was filled with incense. Then at the height of the Easter service, a priest gave everyone three Easter eggs that had been decorated and wrapped in a veil.

"Christ is risen!" the priest proclaimed. And each person, including May, responded: "He is risen indeed!"

Later May reflected on the stirring event: "I was seized then by a moment of spiritual reality: what would it mean for our world if he had not truly risen?"[1]

Reversing the Irreversible

Throughout Scripture we meet a God who intervenes in the most unexpected ways to reverse what seems to be irreversible:

❖ The world was so full of sin it appeared there could never be a new beginning—and then God called Noah.

❖ The promise to Abraham seemed in jeopardy when he and Sarah couldn't have a child—and then God allowed her to conceive in her old age.

❖ God's people looked as if they'd be stuck forever doing hard labor in Egypt—but then God raised up Moses.

❖ An unmarried virgin became pregnant and the object of ridicule—and then an angel announced that the child was God's Son.

The greatest act of God, however, was his resurrection of Jesus Christ from the dead. Paul staked his faith on that act: "If Christ has not been raised, our preaching is useless and so is your faith" (1 Corinthians 15:14).

Peter recalls the drama in his sermon recorded in Acts 3:

> You handed [Jesus] over to be killed, and you disowned him before Pilate, though he had decided to let him go. You disowned the Holy and Righteous One and asked that a murderer be released to you. You killed the author of life (Acts 3:13b-15a).

Death looked like a period. On that Sunday, when rumors that Jesus' body was missing were flying around Jerusalem, even his own disciples couldn't believe it. They were conditioned only to accept the irreversible. But soon they were convinced that this was something new. These same people who had crawled away from Golgotha were found preaching to large crowds in the temple courts. Jesus' death had only been a semicolon: "But God raised him from the dead. We are witnesses of this," Peter explained (v. 15b).

The resurrection of God's Son forever offers the superlative promise of _reversibility_. Nothing—no act of childhood cruelty, no experience of shame or

remorse, no failure, no shattered dream, no physical
or mental disability, not even death—is final!

Those who believe in the resurrecting God can
never again be the same. They believe in pain, but
not ultimate defeat. They believe in death, but not
ultimate despair.

They live with open, honest doubts, fears, and
pains—joining with the whole creation which groans
to be "liberated from its bondage to decay" (Romans
8:21). They are realistic enough to know there's
enough sorrow to stretch from here to the farthest
galaxy. But they also affirm with Jurgen Moltmann,
author of *Theology of Hope*: "God weeps with us so
that we may someday laugh with him." In other
words, we no longer have to believe in irreversibility.
As we live between the first and second comings of
Jesus Christ, we must never lose hope.

What Would It Mean?

My nomination for Most Heretical Typo recently
went to our local newspaper. I had been getting a
little edgy about all the mistakes in my "Daily
Meditation" column, especially since I was doing it
for free at their request.

The worst one, though, came when I ended a
column quoting from the old song, "One step at a
time, dear Savior." But it was printed "One step at a
time, *dead* Savior." It was a resurrection rebuttal!

What difference does it make? Or as Rollo May
asked, "What would it mean?" It meant everything a
couple of years ago as I pulled my daughter in a red
wagon around the quadrangular hallway at
Children's Hospital in Little Rock. We thought she
was dying. How unfair that encephalitis should
strike a child who was already retarded! As Megan

and I made the journey, we saw many parents with
bleary eyes, many siblings with nervous, awkward
laughter, and many kids with IVs and bald heads
trying to be brave. Oh, yes, it makes a difference
whether the Palestinian tomb was occupied or
vacant that morning! It gives us hope that we will
all have a better life in heaven.

It made a huge difference to Dr. Diane Komp. As
a pediatric oncologist, she had a very difficult time
believing in a loving God. But in her book _A Window
to Heaven_ she recounts her pilgrimage to faith, a
pilgrimage that was guided by her tiny patients and
their parents.

For all those who have mourned, it is
terribly relevant that we serve a
resurrecting God.

She tells of visiting with a mother named Eileen.
When this woman's son was diagnosed with leuke-
mia, she enrolled in graduate classes in religious
education, hoping for answers. One day Dr. Komp
noticed some books in their hospital room written by
theologians who were noted for their skepticism.
When asked about them, Eileen explained that she
was taking a course entitled, Is the Resurrection of
Jesus Christ Relevant Today? So, what did she
think? Dr. Komp asked. With great peace and joy,
Eileen looked at her son as he labored to breathe.
With shining eyes she replied, "I know that it's
relevant!"[2]

Saved by a Resurrecting God

For all those who have mourned, it is terribly

relevant that we serve a resurrecting God. For those who've had to sell their houses to pay creditors. For those who've been gutted by a divorce. For those who've stood on a wind-kissed hill to say a final good-bye to a loved one. For those who've faced every day with pain.

"I am the resurrection and the life," says Jesus Christ (John 11:25). Either he is or he isn't. It depends on what happened that weekend in Palestine. For those like me who believe that he was raised by his Father, there is wild hope. Suffering and death do not have the final word!

Jesus died, but he conquered sin and death with his resurrection so we may live and be victorious in life.

And we, like Mary, will live through to the resurrection! Life did not end at the Cross! All is not lost just because it seems so at times. We too will have our day of resurrection! Jesus died, but he conquered sin and death with his resurrection so we may live and be victorious in life. Now that same power that raised him and seated him at the Father's right hand is available to us (Ephesians 1:19). We don't have to be conquered by sin—by the temper, rage, and detestable behaviors that can well up inside us when things go wrong. We only need to utilize the power he has already given to us!

Scripture promises us that Jesus' blood has redeemed us from our empty way of life—possibly the life that we were given by our parents (1 Peter 1:18). Life is not irreversible because he has given us the power to change.

When Winston Churchill's funeral was held at
Saint Paul's Cathedral in London, the service was
conducted according to his instructions. After the
blessing, a bugler positioned high in the dome played
taps, signaling the end of the day. But after that, a
bugler on the other side played reveille, signaling a
new day has begun. "Sleeper, awake! Rise from the
dead, and Christ will shine on you" (Ephesians
5:14b).

What a glorious morning that will be! It is the
time when those who have hungered and thirsted for
the presence of God will be filled beyond imagina-
tion. It is the time when this God for whom we
hunger, the resurrecting God, will call—and all the
universe will answer.

Notes:

1. Written by Rollo May, reported by Philip Yancey, "Friends
Are Friends Forever," _Campus Life_.

2. Diane Komp, _A Window to Heaven_ (Grand Rapids:
Zondervan, 1992).

Focusing Your Faith

1. Suppose you heard this chapter preached as a sermon. How would you summarize it for a friend who was not present? What ideas would you choose to share?

2. How does the resurrection of Jesus show who is really in control here?

3. How can other people tell by your actions that you believe Jesus is alive?

4. Tell a friend about a time in your life you have been comforted by faith in the Resurrection.

5. What have you wished you'd never said or done to someone? If you haven't gone to that person, why not do it now? Then pray that God will release you from your feelings of guilt.

6. Reflect on a seemingly irreversible situation in your life—a time things seemed they couldn't be worse. Identify ways that you now believe God actually turned things around for you.

7. What songs would you request for your own funeral which symbolize your feelings about life and death?

Chapter 13

Discover:

The Perfect

Imprint of God

I've been trying to paint a more complete picture of God through the descriptions of him in Scripture. It's like being at the optometrist's office. Each click of the lens brings the eye chart into a little better focus as the

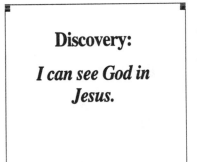

Discovery:

I can see God in Jesus.

optometrist searches for the perfect prescription. The goal is to help people see with 20/20 vision.

Since I'm nearsighted, I have the same experience nearly every time I jog alone. I hate it when I greet someone from a distance only to find out that the person is actually a mailbox! The closer I get, the more clearly I see.

With our blurred vision, God can look terribly out of focus. People begin to see him as a policeman, as a parent who can't be pleased, as an angry principal, as a pushover grandparent, or as a respectable member of the middle class.

We've put on the contact lenses of Scripture to see him more clearly. As we looked at some of the pictures of God—father, mother, spouse, shepherd— and some of his attributes, this biblical perspective improves our view of him.

But in this final chapter, I want to remind you that there is one picture of God that is clearer than all the others, one that knows no limitation. It is the image of God imprinted in the person of Jesus Christ.

Jesus of Nazareth gave concrete

expression to the invisible God.

Parents can't really explain the concept of "red" to a toddler. It doesn't help to drag out Webster: "Honey, red is a color whose hue is that of the long- wave extreme of the visible spectrum." Rather, parents point to a red ball and say "red." And then to an apple. And then to a sweater. The child eventu- ally figures out redness by looking at and handling red objects.

We are all influenced by our visual impressions. That's why cafeterias make a killing off of bright red Jello and strawberry shortcake. Even if we're not hungry in the car, when we walk up to the line and catch a glimpse of those brilliant desserts, suddenly we're starving. It's the same way with our spiritual hunger. When we catch a glimpse of the Person of Jesus, his magnificence whets our appetites and we hunger even more to know God.

A Clear Picture

"In the beginning was the Word, and the Word was with God, and the Word was God" (John 1:1). Hundreds of thousands of pages have been written about John's use of the word *logos* ("word"). There are many possibilities from Old Testament and Greek backgrounds.

Part of the explanation may be that a word gives concrete expression to a thought. How do I know what's floating around in your mind until you translate those thoughts into words? When you share those words with me, I can begin to understand.

Similarly, Jesus of Nazareth gave concrete expression to the invisible God. Even though no one has ever seen God, this Son of God came from the Father's side to make him known to us (John 1:18). He is the revealer of God. Through him we obtain our clearest and truest account of who God is and what he's like.

Jesus Is the Place

According to John, the Incarnation—God in human form—was more than just a necessary preliminary to the crucifixion. Jesus also came to reveal God to us.

He said to the early followers, "I tell you the truth, you shall see heaven open, and the angels of God ascending and descending on the Son of Man" (John 1:51). Jesus is referring to the well-known dream of Jacob at Bethel:

[Jacob] had a dream in which he saw a stairway resting on the earth, with its top reaching to heaven, and the angels of God were ascending and descending on it. . . . When Jacob awoke from his sleep, he thought, "Surely the LORD is in this place, and I was not aware of it." He was afraid and said, "How awesome is this place! This is none other than the house of God; this is the gate of heaven" (Genesis 28:12, 16).

Jesus claims to be the place where we meet God! He told the Pharisees later, "If you knew me, you would know my Father" (John 8:19). And when Philip asked him to show the disciples the Father, Jesus replied:

Don't you know me, Philip, even after I have been among you such a long time? Anyone who has seen me has seen the Father. How could you say, "Show us the Father"? Don't you believe that I am in the Father, and that the Father is in me? The words I say to you are not just my own. Rather, it is the Father, living in me, who is doing his work. Believe me when I say that I am in the Father and the Father is in me (John 14:9-11a).

Jesus Is the Face

Most people know Augustine as "Saint Augustine," the brilliant mind who devoted his life to Christ in the fourth and fifth centuries. But he wasn't born a "saint." At one point Augustine wondered how a perfect, incorruptible God could put up with an oversexed, undisciplined person like himself. He tried various religious experiments and found them all unsatisfactory. Then he discovered the Jesus of the Gospels and saw the caring and accepting God whom Jesus revealed.

In 1967, Joni Eareckson Tada was an active, athletic teenager. But then a diving accident left her

a quadriplegic. Times of anger and resentment set in
as she struggled for faith. Three years after the
accident, one of her closest friends, sitting by her
bed, spoke of Jesus and how "he was paralyzed too."
He, too, was paralyzed by bearing his strength in the
form of weakness. "He was crucified in weakness,
yet he lives by God's power" (2 Corinthians 13:4a).
Though Jesus had all the power, he yielded to the
will of God, dying an unfair death on the cross. That
moment, she later wrote, was a turning point in her
life. Through Jesus she could see a God who cared
deeply about her and who understood what it was
like to be paralyzed.

> _Jesus didn't bring a tender edge to_
> _the wrath of God. . . . He revealed the_
> _God that_ is _love._

Let's never fall into the trap of thinking that
Jesus softened God up a bit, as some medieval
descriptions of the atonement make it sound. Jesus
didn't bring a tender edge to the wrath of God.
Rather, he revealed the loving heart that God has
had from eternity. He revealed the God that _is_ love.

Jesus Is the Grace

When we see Jesus our vision of God begins to
come into focus. We learn from this One who came
from above (John 3:13, 31; 6:33, 38; 7:29) what the
Father is like.

As he turns the water into wine, as he heals the
sick, as he claims power over nature, and as he even
raises the dead, we catch a glimpse of the power of
God Almighty.

As he storms into the temple area, driving people and animals out and kicking over tables, screaming, "How dare you turn my Father's house into a market!" we learn how irreverence and hypocrisy enrage the Lord.

As he deals so tenderly with people whose lives are broken, offering salvation and challenging them to a new life, we see the compassion of God.

As he kneels to wash ten toes of each disciple (including Judas), we learn again the nature of a serving God.

How should we treat people who are handicapped or hypocritical or lonely or divorced or mixed up? Watch intently as you read through John's gospel to see how God treated them—and how he treats each of us!

Jesus Is Eternal Life

In her book *Up With Worship*, Anne Ortlund pictures a small child looking through the knothole of a fence to see a parade. The child sees a clown, then horses, then a lion. He enjoys each part, but really has no perspective on the parade. Suppose, though, that a kind-hearted man picks him up so that he can see over the fence. Then he catches a view of the whole parade.[1]

Jesus is like that kind-hearted man as he holds us up for a better view of God.

Jesus is like that kind-hearted man as he holds us up for a better view of God. Through the life and ministry of Jesus Christ we have been allowed to see the glory of the Father. Just as importantly, through his work we are permitted to experience full, abundant life (John 10:10).

But this eternal life which Christ's followers possess isn't anything like the "abundant life" depicted on television soap operas. Jesus was clear that it is much more than that:

> Now this is eternal life: that they may know you, the only true God, and Jesus Christ, whom you have sent (John 17:3).

Come and Be Filled

This brings us back to where we began: to souls panting for God, to men and women hungering for the Lord, to people longing to know intimately their Creator and Redeemer.

Each time he gave us a picture of himself, God helped us understand him more so we could love him more. Each time he revealed one of his qualities, we had more to praise. But it is in Jesus Christ that we see the one true God most clearly.

Now we can focus better on this One who deserves and demands our time, our money, our devotion, and our hearts so that we can be transformed each day more fully into his likeness. Now through Jesus, the Bread of Life, we who are filled with this one holy hunger can be filled with his presence.

John Ortberg has written that slick television advertising has made his children believe that their little souls have a McDonald's-shaped vacuum. "Our hearts are restless till they find their rest in a Happy Meal," they think.

Many people approach their spiritual hunger in a similar way. They allow the influences around them to dictate what they diet on. Unfortunately, the spiritual junk food many have turned to will no more nourish their souls than a Happy Meal. They binge on this diet but remain spiritually empty.

What they—we—are craving is the God who created us in his image. God designed each of us with an inborn desire that can only be satisfied with the healing, utterly satisfying food of his presence in our souls. Our God-given hunger draws us to him for the cleansing, completing, enfolding warmth of his love and acceptance.

The ravenous hunger inside the human soul cannot be filled by mere information about God. Imagine a starving man, his cheeks sunken and his ribs protruding. With his last strength he crawls into a restaurant. He painfully drags himself up to the counter. Then he pulls a pad and pencil out of his pocket and begins to copy down the menu, carefully noting each entree and its cost.

Ridiculous! The man is starving! He doesn't need to know *about* the food—he needs to eat it! And yet, for many of us, the quest to fill the emptiness in our hearts begins and ends with a cataloging of God's attributes, the facts and figures of his dealings with biblical people, and a tally of his rules and regulations.

But there is so much more. There is a loving Father who has gone through the adoption procedures and is waiting for us to accept him as our Father. There is an eternal Mother who longs to embrace you. There is an All-Knowing Mate who is intimately acquainted with your needs. There is a Shepherd who has walked the same roads and tasted the same tears and endured the same pains as you and me—all so that he could show us the way. And there is a God of grace who has given up everything—even his own life—to save you.

God knows you personally and wants you to know him. And you, whether you realize it or not, want and desperately need to know God. You want to live a life of purpose, filled with his presence. He has prepared a table for you. The feast is ready. If you're hungry . . . come and be filled.

Notes:

1. Anne Ortlund, _Up with Worship_ (Ventura: Regal Books, 1982).

Focusing Your Faith

1. How does the life and ministry of Jesus help you
    to see God more clearly? Choose your favorite
    story of Jesus in the Gospels and tell how you
    think that story reveals what God is like.

2. Ask yourself, Why was I born? Have you discov-
    ered yet what God's plans are for your life?

3. Think of a time when you've been very hungry—
    how did you feel inside? Did the hunger control
    your actions? Do you feel hungry for the Lord
    with that same intensity?

4. What do you see as the key to solving our prob-
    lem of "world hunger"?

5. What steps can you take in order to know God
    better?

6. Set a goal for this week that will increase your
    knowledge of God.

7. In light of what you've read in this book, how
    would you now answer the question, What hun-
    ger causes you the greatest pain in your daily
    living?